Saints of California

Saints of California

A Guide to Places and Their Patrons

Edward and Lorna Mornin

For Trish and Hannes —
with very best wishes,
Eddie   Lorna

THE J. PAUL GETTY MUSEUM
LOS ANGELES

Published by the J. Paul Getty Museum, Los Angeles

Copyright © Frances Lincoln Limited 2009
Text © Edward and Lorna Mornin 2009

Getty Publications
1200 Getty Center Drive, Suite 500
Los Angeles, California 90049-1682
www.getty.edu/publications

Gregory M. Britton, *Publisher*
Mark Greenberg, *Editor in Chief*
Ann Lucke, *Managing Editor*
Mollie Holtman, *Editor*

Library of Congress Cataloging-in-Publication Data

Mornin, Edward.
  Saints of California : a guide to places and their patrons / Edward and
Lorna Mornin.
    p. cm.
  Includes bibliographical references and index.
  ISBN 978-0-89236-984-3 (paper)
  1. Christian patron saints--California. 2. Christian patron
saints--Biography. 3. Names, Geographical--California. 4. Historic
sites--California. 5. California--History, Local. 6.
California--History--To 1846. I. Mornin, Lorna. II. Title.
  BX4659.U5M67 2009
  282.092'2794--dc22
                                    2009019595

FRONT COVER *The Blessing of the Consuls of Bevagna and Montefalco* (Detail from
Scenes from the Life of St Francis). Fresco, 1452, by Benozzo Gozzoli. Church of San
Francesco, Montefalco, Italy. Courtesy of Scala/Art Resource, NY.

BACK COVER *St Monica*. Icon, 2000, by Sister Marie-Paul Farran, O.S.B. Church of
St Monica, Santa Monica, California.

HALF-TITLE PAGE *St Marinus*. Fresco, early sixteenth century, by School of
Ghirlandaio. Courtesy of the Museo di Stato della Repubblica di San Marino. The
saint holds the city he is said to have founded.

TITLE PAGE *St Luke*, with his emblem of a winged bull. Stained-glass window in the
chapel of the Dominican Sisters at Mission San Jose, Fremont, California.

CONTENTS

INTRODUCTION

Californians may understandably wonder from time to time who exactly were all those "San"s and "Santa"s that pepper the map of their state. And visitors may be forgiven for asking just how in the first place so many Christian saints came to adorn California's landscape anyway. Certainly, an immediately striking feature of California geography is the frequency in it of locations named for saints. They have left their mark on hills and mountains, on rivers, lakes, and streams, on bays and straits, and on headlands and islands, as well as on cities, towns, and villages.

Californians are proudly conscious of their historical and cultural heritage, not least of its Spanish and Mexican components, conspicuous signs of which are evident in the state's ubiquitous mission architecture and Spanish place names. On occasion, it is true, commentators have regretted what they judge the indiscriminate application of so many saints' names in the state. Hence, Edwin G. Gudde (xii) can write: "One might even be inclined to agree with Mark Twain and Walt Whitman that too many saints' names in California were applied in a purely mechanical manner and not because of any association with the natural, social, or political history of the places named."

One need not necessarily accept this view. On the most basic level, residents and visitors alike have every right to savor the state's many mellifluous saints' names and to delight in their aura of hidden narratives and of a culture of faith distant from the often fast and hard-edged world of modern California. Beyond that, as will be seen, these names not infrequently do tell something of interest about a location – not only the day of its naming, for instance, but at other times considerably more about the circumstances attending its discovery. Above all, the saints behind the names are themselves worthy of attention. Even the least of them has his or her own story to tell, and frequently occupies a significant place in the political, religious, social, or art history of Europe, especially of Spain, from where California's first European settlers came. This is not to belittle the contribution of earlier native, or later non-European, settlers to the culture of the state – though it is worth recalling that many of California's newest immigrants, originating from Catholic, Spanish-speaking Mexico, feel close affinities to its saintly place names.

With only a few exceptions, California's saints go back in one way or another to the early explorations and foundations of presidios, missions, chapels, ranches, and pueblos by Spanish soldiers and friars and to subsequent namings (e.g., of land grants) by Mexican governors. Hence, the most important phases of Spanish exploration and settlement and the reasons for them deserve to be set out briefly here. The English, Russians, and Americans also left their mark on California's names, of course, and these will be treated as appropriate in the text.

One must first bear in mind that early California lay in the extreme northwest of Spanish America, on the very edge of that vastness claimed for Spain by right of conquest and of a 1493 Papal Bull of Alexander VI. It was actually not until the beginning of the eighteenth century that Lower (Baja) California was indisputably accepted to be a peninsula, not an island, and that today's Upper (or Alta) California was known to form part of the American mainland. Baja California had already been sparsely colonized by Spain, and Jesuit missions had been established among the natives there, before exploration of Alta California properly began.

The initial exploration of what is today California took place, along the coastline only, from the sea. At the Viceroy of Mexico's command, the navigator Juan Rodríguez Cabrillo sailed north along the coast in 1542, principally charged with finding the Strait of Anián, that waterway linking Europe to Asia known in English as the North-West Passage. Though unsuccessful in his quest, Cabrillo discovered and named many features on the coast. Virtually all of these were renamed by later explorers, however, notably by Sebastián Vizcaíno in his naval explorations of 1602–03. Ambitious and self-promoting, Vizcaíno thus papered over Cabrillo's considerable earlier achievements. Venturing as far north as today's border with Oregon, Vizcaíno left an indelible mark on the state's names. Yet his voyage did not set the scene for colonization of any sort. At this period, Spain saw no advantage in settling what they viewed as a profitless territory, devoid of wealthy cities or mines (unlike Mexico or Peru). Moreover, given the prevailing contrary coastal winds, maritime access to California from Mexico was extremely time-consuming and arduous, fraught with the perils of shipwreck and of death by scurvy for sailors.

It was only toward the end of the eighteenth century, when they felt their northwestern American claims were being challenged by the advances southward of Russians (via Alaska) and the British (by sea, and by land through Canada), that the Spaniards determined to plant settlements in today's California. These plans were then realized primarily though land expeditions, first for exploration, then for conducting colonists and livestock from Mexico to the new territories. Support from the sea remained vital in the early years, however, as the young settlements long remained far from being self-sufficient.

The first land expedition from Mexico, departing from Baja California, took place in 1769 under the overall command of army Captain Gaspar de Portolá (second-in-command, Fernando de Rivera y Moncada). Two segments of the expedition (led by Moncada and Portolá respectively) successfully reached San Diego, where they met up with two supply ships likewise dispatched from Baja California. (A third ship was lost at sea.) The long-term purpose of these undertakings was political, military, economic, and religious. The Spanish wished to defend their American possessions against foreign incursions and at the same time to develop a coastal base to service and protect Spanish merchant galleons sailing between Manila in the Philippines and Acapulco in Mexico. A much publicized, though not exclusively altruistic, aspiration, too, was to Christianize the California native Indian population – in conformity with a long-standing practice of the Spaniards in their American possessions. The natives were intended, in fact, to play a vital part in securing California for Spain. Through their conversion and their training in useful crafts, they were to form what were in essence "Spanish" communities grouped around mission churches and settlements.

Spanish priests were, therefore, active from the outset in California. Though it has been argued that their treatment of the Indians was harsh, their enormous contribution to the social and economic development of the region is undisputed. They not only built missions and attended to the Indians' religious education, but were fully involved in the practicalities of instructing them in a wide variety of trades, including carpentry, construction, agriculture, herding, leatherwork, and the like. This missionary task was entrusted to the Franciscan Order, and it was Franciscans such as Fathers Junípero Serra, Francisco Palóu, Fermín de Lasuén, and Juan Crespí that named so many of California's places for saints. The first three of these priests served consecutively as Franciscan President in the years 1769 to 1803 and were responsible for founding many of the important missions.

Portolá's soldiers and their missionary companions named many places en route from Baja California northward as they blazed the trail of what later became known as El Camino Real. They also established presidios and missions at San Diego (1769) and Monterey (1770), and ventured as far north as present-day San Francisco Bay, which was in 1769 first sighted and "discovered" from land by José Francisco de Ortega, a sergeant of Portolá's party.

In view of the moral authority of the Franciscan fathers in all of these undertakings, many place designations commemorated the saint on whose feast day a name was given, or a favorite saint near whose day a name was given – perhaps to a campsite, to a river that had to be crossed, or to a mountain that served as a landmark. (A religious "feast day" is the day of the year on which the Church officially commemorates a saint, usually the date of his or her death.) Formally or informally, these saints may still be regarded as the patrons of the places they name.

Despite Portolá's successes, the overland supply route from Baja to Alta California proved to be impracticable in the long run, for Baja California itself had to be supplied by sea from the Mexican mainland port of San Blas. Hence, army Captain Juan Bautista de Anza, commanding two separate parties, in 1774 and 1775–76, was commissioned to open up a new land route northward from Sonora, on the northwestern Mexican mainland. By this time, he was able to count on a measure of support and assistance from the soldiers and missionaries already in California and stationed at San Diego, Monterey (Mission San Carlos), and San Gabriel. Overcoming all setbacks, Anza proved brilliantly successful. The culmination of his work was the foundation in 1776 of San Francisco presidio (supervised by his second-in-command, José Joaquín Moraga) and of Mission San Francisco (dedicated by Father Palóu) in the same year.

By 1776, within only seven years, the remarkable efforts of Portolá and Anza and their attendant Franciscans had already established (at San Diego, Monterey, and San Francisco) three out of the final total of four California presidios and, in all, seven missions. From these achievements, and from further explorations and missionary activities (such as the establishment of branch missions and ranches), evolved much of the early nomenclature of the state. Later, the foundation of new missions, to a total of twenty-one by 1823, and the conducting of forays into the interior (notably under Lieutenant Gabriel Moraga in the years 1805–17), added further Spanish names to the territory. Spanish control never extended far north of Sonoma, however, accounting for the vast preponderance of Hispanic names in the southern part of today's state. Correspondingly, the English spelling of some saints' names is more likely to occur in the northern part of the state, as in Saint Catherine Creek or Saint Charles Hill in Sierra County.

More new names appeared on the map of California through the awarding of properties to individuals (land grants) by the Spanish and later the Mexican authorities. Mexico, it should be remembered, became fully independent of Spain in 1822, with important repercussions for California. Originally, the Franciscan mission lands were intended to be secularized and turned over to the Indians after only ten years. In fact, however, it was not until Mexico supplanted Spain in California that secularization began. It was then carried out, after 1834, in a highly improper manner, as few mission lands ever did revert to the native peoples who had, with Franciscan guidance, created them in the first place. Instead, sometimes vast tracts were signed over to retired soldiers, recent settlers, or (often as not) already wealthy, high-placed California-born Mexicans (Californios). During the Mexican era, before the short period of California independence (1846) and eventual statehood (1850), close to seven hundred such land grants were approved. Most of these received saints' names, in part out of tradition, no doubt, but in part perhaps to lend a stamp of propriety or rightness to a corrupt and unjust process.

After the advent of the Americans, the state's Spanish names were generally retained, though, as will be seen, a few were altered somewhat. Others were even added, and a number of older ones from land grants were revived. Today still, Spanish-sounding names, including saints' names, are not infrequently given to new sub-divisions, schools, wineries, streets, and the like.

California's saints form a motley company. To be sure, many of them were either Spaniards or Franciscan friars (or both) during their lifetimes, thus revealing a certain predilection on the part of the Franciscan fathers. Many, however, are non-Spanish, may be women as well as men, and Biblical or legendary as well as historical. A few, such as Gorgonius and Carpophorus, are scarcely known today at all. Most, however, are familiar or, indeed, either historically famous or celebrated through great works of European art from the Middle Ages or the Renaissance to more modern times.

We, the authors, have pursued in the text and illustrations of this book a time-honored two-fold purpose: to instruct and to please (Horace's "*docere et delectare*"). We have sketched the historical origin for each place name treated, to the extent it is known. Though aiming for adequate coverage in this, we have also tried to avoid informational overkill. We hope to have mentioned all major, and many minor, instances of a saint's name in California, but do not aspire to completeness, which is the proper purpose of a *gazetteer*.[1] We have also limited ourselves to present-day communities and (with only a few exceptions) to today's names for natural landscape features – omitting much reference to schools, churches, ranches, dams, wineries, and the like. Nor do we dwell on the names of spurious saints, despite the interesting etymology of some, such as Santa Nella, San Sevaine, or Santa Venetia.[2] In the matter of fictitious saints, Bancroft (II 598 footnote 25) alludes to the tendency of new American settlers in California, possibly knowing little Spanish, to insert a "San" in front of everything. This led to the possibility that at some point one might hear Mt Diablo (*diablo* meaning devil in Spanish) referred to as Mt San Diablo!

In our discussion of place name origins, we gratefully acknowledge our indebtedness to the laborious work of others. Especially Gudde's *California Place Names* (4th edition by William Bright) has proven indispensable. Reference is made to Gudde and others, however, only

---

[1] See David L. Durham's *California's Geographic Names. A Gazetteer of Historic and Modern Names of the State* (Word Dancer Press: Clovis, California, 1998).

[2] Santa Nella (Merced County) is probably an imaginative corruption of Spanish *Centinela* (=Sentinel). San Sevaine Flats (San Bernardino County) is a hispanicism for Sainsevain, the name of an early French pioneer. Santa Venetia (Marin County) was originally intended to resemble Venice in Italy.

where specifics call for some sort of comment. Historical background data have been garnered from a range of histories, not least from Bancroft's *History of California*, while Hart's *Companion to California* has served as an ever-handy reference source. Beyond that, municipal, county, state, and federal topographical and demographic documents available on the Internet have provided much up-to-date reference material. The most useful books consulted are acknowledged in our Select Bibliography on page 187–188.

As to our documentation of saints' lives and legends, many works have proven helpful, including Butler's multi-volume *Lives of the Saints* and Farmer's compact *Dictionary of Saints*. We have benefited, too, from the preparation of our own book on the subject, our recent *Saints: A Visual Guide*. For further information on individual saints, readers are directed to works listed in the bibliography.

The saints we discuss here could, almost without exception, benefit from fuller treatment, but in the interests of concision we have limited ourselves in most instances to a brief overview. To enliven our narrative and expand our frame of reference, however, we have provided illustrations of the saints as available. In so doing, we have used a good image from California wherever possible. This includes images of works by present-day artists, demonstrating that the saints may provide an important source of inspiration for creative people today still. At the same time, to provide variety, we have also selected other images from "compatible" sources, in Mexico or Spain. Beyond that, we have on occasion gladly used images from churches or galleries in other European countries or the United States. We hope through this not only to add variety and appeal to our work, but to show how, in its place names, California has links with the treasures of the European past, to which (among other riches) it is heir. Ultimately, our aim, through text and pictures, has been to proceed from local particulars of everyday California experience to an enrichment of our readers through exposure to the great stream of Western historical, narrative, and artistic tradition.

PLACES AND THEIR PATRONS

Entries are listed alphabetically according to the
present-day Spanish (or debased Spanish, or English)
form of the saint's portion of a place name (e.g., Santa
Ana before San Andreas; Saint George before San
Geronimo). Places that do not have a San or Santa in
their name are inserted alphabetically into this scheme
(e.g., Los Angeles before Saint Louis).

SAN AGUSTIN
(ST AUGUSTINE)

Perhaps California's early Franciscan missionaries felt that the intellectual St Augustine (Spanish: Agustín) would have shared little concern for the gritty particulars of everyday life they generally had to contend with. Certainly, despite his prominence as one of the Church's most eminent scholars and theologians, he has left few marks on the state's place names. There is, however, a San Agustin Creek, in Santa Cruz County – not officially recorded until 1854, long after the mission period. In Santa Barbara County, there are also a San Augustin Canyon and a San Augustine (English spelling) settlement.

Augustine was actually late in turning to religion. Born in Tagaste in Roman North Africa in 354, he grew up a loose-living free thinker, despite the efforts of his mother Monica (later herself canonized) to convert him to Christianity. However, he early established himself as a brilliant lawyer, philosopher, and teacher, in Rome and later in Milan. He also lived for fifteen years with a mistress, by whom he had a son. His disapproval of his own youthful worldly life emerges in his *Confessions*, written after his conversion at the age of thirty-three and regarded as the earliest autobiography in Western literature. Due to his intellectual powers and organizational abilities, he was, after his ordination as a priest, soon appointed Bishop of Hippo in North Africa, where he died in 430. Other important writings by Augustine were his *City of God* and *On the Trinity*. For his erudition he was declared one of the Latin Doctors of the Church.

St Augustine. Mural, *c.*1938, by Ettore Serbaroli, Church of St Monica, Santa Monica, California.

SANTA ANA
(ST ANNE)

Given her prominence as the mother of the Virgin Mary, St Anne fittingly occurs in many names in the state. The Santa Ana River, in San Bernardino, Riverside, and Orange Counties, received its name from soldiers of Portolá's Mexico-California overland expedition as early as July 28, 1769, two days after her feast day. Apart from the modern city of Santa Ana, on the south bank of the river, there are also a Santa Ana Canyon and Mountains in Orange County. The Santa Ana is the name, too, for the hot dry wind that fans summer fires in southern California.

St Anne is present, further, in the name of Anaheim, Orange County. German settlers named it in 1857 for the Santa Ana River plus "-heim" (German for "home"). Likewise transformed, she appears in Santa Anita ("little Santa Ana"), a horse race track in Los Angeles County. Santa Ana occurs as a place name also in San Benito and Ventura Counties.

Nothing is known with certainty about Anne, the mother of Jesus's own mother. Even her name is a matter of tradition, not of historical record, as she was first mentioned in the second-century apocryphal (i.e. noncanonical) gospel of James. It is assumed, however, that she was an exemplary mother to Mary. In art, as in the accompanying illustration, she is often depicted teaching the young Mary to read.

St Anne. Ex Convento de San Bernardino de Siena, Taxco, Mexico.

ABCD
EFGH
IJKLM

SAN ANDREAS
(ST ANDREW)

The name Andreas is celebrated, if not notorious, in California for its association with the San Andreas Fault, the state's major earthquake zone, which was itself named in 1893 after the San Andreas Valley, through which it runs in San Mateo County. The valley received its name from Father Francisco Palóu, journeying from Monterey to San Francisco, on November 30 (St Andrew's Day) 1774. There is also a San Andreas Lake in the county. Interestingly, the Spanish form of Andrew is Andrés, not Andreas, which is the Latin form. The name Andreas was not used during the Spanish or Mexican eras, but was introduced by the Americans, who presumably felt more familiar with this form than with the Spanish.

The small town of San Andreas, county seat of Calaveras County in the Sierra foothills, was settled and named by Mexican gold miners around 1848.

Andrew, a fisherman, was the first disciple Jesus called to him (according to John 1: 40–42), and as such he enjoys a certain prominence among the twelve. It was he, too, who brought his younger brother Peter, also a fisherman, to Jesus, who thus made them "fishers of men." Tradition relates that after the crucifixion Andrew preached the gospel in Greece. Patras in Greece claims to be the scene of his martyrdom, when he was allegedly crucified on a diagonal cross, today generally known as a "St Andrew's Cross." He is a patron saint of Scotland, Russia, and Greece.

St Andrew. Oil on canvas, late eighteenth century, Mexican. With kind permission of Mission San Juan Bautista, San Juan Bautista, California.

SAN ANSELMO
(ST ANSELM)

Anselm was a monk and bishop of considerable importance for the history of the Church in England. Yet as a place designation San Anselmo illustrates how such names may occasionally be only indirectly linked to actual saints in California. San Anselmo Valley, in Marin County, was at first, in 1840, called simply Cañada de Anselmo, apparently after an Indian who had received the name on baptism. The "San" was added at a later date, no doubt to conform to similar California place names, and the valley then gave its name to today's town.

Anselm's biography neatly exemplifies the international character of the European Church in his day. Though born in 1033 in Aosta, Italy, he lived the greater part of his life as a Benedictine monk in France and ultimately rose to become Archbishop of Canterbury, England in 1093. As archbishop he had no easy tenure, for during his episcopacy he came into frequent conflict with the English king over the jurisdictional powers of State and Church. It was he, however, who established the primacy of Canterbury over all other archdioceses in England. He also distinguished himself as a theologian, in which capacity he is best remembered for his "ontological" proof of God's existence.

St Anselm. Stained glass, 1957, by A. K. Nicholson Studios. Church of St Giles Cripplegate, London. As one can see, Anselm's emblem is a hare. Tradition relates that he once saved a hare from hunters, seeing it as an analogy for the human soul pursued by devils.

SAN ANTONIO
(ST ANTHONY)

Though history knows two prominent St Anthonys, Anthony the Great (also known as Anthony Abbot) and Anthony of Padua, it was probably the latter, one of the most important Franciscans, that California's many San Antonios commemorate. Father Junípero Serra, the first President of California's Franciscan missionaries, gave the name in 1771 to the river and probably also the valley in today's Monterey County. In the valley lies Mission San Antonio de Padua, founded also by Serra in 1771 as the third of California's missions. Still located in an isolated setting today, the reconstructed church and its outbuildings convey a good impression to the visitor of how the mission might have looked in Spanish times.

The name San Antonio is prominent, too, in San Bernardino County, being applied to San Antonio Mountains and Mount San Antonio, as well as to a creek and canyon and the modern community of San Antonio Heights.

Mission San Antonio de Pala was named for the Pala Indians and stands on today's Pala Indian Reservation in San Diego County. Founded in 1816 as an *asistencia* (branch mission) of San Luis Rey, it is the only Spanish mission to survive in its original purpose of service to the Native American Indians.

Numerous other locations and natural features are named for St Anthony – for example, in Ventura, Sonoma, Marin, Santa Barbara, Calaveras, Alameda, and Santa Clara Counties.

Born in Lisbon, Portugal around 1195, Anthony's ambition, after becoming a Franciscan, was actually to serve as a missionary in North Africa. Attendance at a Franciscan General-Chapter in Italy in 1221, however, convinced him that he ought to dedicate himself to the advancement of his order in Europe. He spent the rest of his life in Italy and France, earning a reputation as the foremost preacher of his age. Legend relates that at Rimini on Italy's Adriatic coast Anthony's preaching attracted a multitude of little fishes to the shore to hear him – hence converting his human listeners who had thus far listened to no good effect. Anthony's eloquent tongue is preserved as a relic in the Basilica of Il Santo in Padua, Italy, where he died in 1231. He was declared a saint in less than a year, the fastest canonization on record.

St Anthony of Padua, preaching to the fishes. Mural.
With kind permission of San Antonio de Padua, California.

SAN ARDO
See SAN BERNARDO

SANTA BARBARA
(ST BARBARA)

Santa Barbara (Spanish: Bárbara) is one of the early saints' names of California. On his historic voyage of exploration north along the coast, Sebastián Vizcaíno applied it to Santa Barbara Channel and Island on her feast day of December 4, 1602. The name was subsequently given to the presidio (California's fourth and last) in 1782 and to the mission, founded on December 4, 1786. Today's splendid church (popularly known as the "Queen of the Missions") was the tenth of California's twenty-one and was founded by Father Fermín de Lasuén (the first of the nine he dedicated as then President of the Franciscans). It is the only mission to have remained continuously under Franciscan control for religious purposes from Spanish times until the present. Modern Santa Barbara city and county were created in 1850. The four Santa Barbara Islands lie twenty-five to thirty miles offshore.

Barbara was for centuries one of the most venerated women saints because of her many patronages – for example, to name a few, of architects, miners, artillerymen, stonemasons, milliners, and those who live in constant danger of sudden death. Her life, however, has been deemed entirely legendary by Church scholars, so that since 1969 she has been deleted from the Roman Calendar of Saints. This, of course, in no way diminishes her importance as a subject in art, for she has been depicted by, among others, Caravaggio, Ghirlandaio, Jan van Eyck, Dürer, and Holbein. According to her legend, the beautiful Barbara lived in some part of the Roman Empire toward the end of the third century and was confined to a tower by her pagan father in order to shield her from the attentions of men. During one of his absences, Barbara converted to Christianity and, in honor of the Holy Trinity, had a third window built into her tower. Discovering this on his return, her father (cruel father!) denounced her to the Roman magistrate, who commanded him to kill his daughter with a sword. After he did so, the father was himself struck dead by a bolt of lightening.

Saint Barbara, with her tower. Illumination from *Spinola Hours*. Flemish, *c.*1510–20. Courtesy of the J. Paul Getty Museum, Los Angeles, California.

SAN BENANCIO
(ST VENANTIUS)

Venantius is today a little known saint whose memory has been preserved since the 1830s in Monterey County's San Benancio Gulch. According to Gudde (330), the name may honor one of four recorded St Venantiuses, in which case its likely inspiration was Venantius Fortunatus, the relatively most prominent of the four.

Born in Italy about 530, Venantius lived most of his life in France, where he became Bishop of Poitiers around 600 and where he died at the advanced age of eighty. A distinguished writer and poet, his works include prose and verse versions of Lives of Saints, as well as church hymns. Among these, his most enduring success was his "*Vexilla regis prodeunt.*" John Mason Neale has translated this into English as "The royal banners forward go" (1854). It is sung today to the melody of "Hamburg" (1825), composed by Lowell Mason. Legend asserts that St. Radegund presented the city of Poitiers with a fragment of what was believed to be the True Cross and that Venantius was chosen to receive it on its arrival. When the bearers of the relic were some distance from the city, Venantius, with a great number of believers, some carrying banners, advanced to meet them. As they marched, they sang this hymn that the saint had composed.

Venantius Fortunatus Reading His Poems to Radegonda. Oil on canvas, 1862, by Lawrence Alma-Tadema. This striking, and rather sultry, Pre-Raphaelite painting hangs in Dordrechts Museum, Dordrecht, Netherlands.

SAN BENITO
(ST BENEDICT)

Benedict, who has been called the "father of Western monasticism," is commemorated by the San Benito Valley (named by Father Juan Crespí in 1772), as well as by the river, mountain, and location of the name. All of these being in San Benito County, this represents a remarkably concentrated memorial to a person whose influence has been so far-reaching.

Benedict was the founder of the earliest European monastic order, called for him the Benedictines. Hence, he was in a sense the originator of all those orders that shaped medieval European culture and which still play an important part in the religious, educational, and social life of to-day's world. He was born around 480 in Norcia, Umbria and, after years of withdrawal from the world, established with a body of like-minded men his famous monastery of Monte Cassino in southern Italy about 530. This became the motherhouse for all future Benedictine monasteries. Like most other saints, Benedict is the focus of numerous legends (see illustration), but these are overshadowed in his case by his real historical importance.

St Benedict. Oil on canvas (detail). Holy Chapel of Misericordia, Braga, Portugal. He wears the black habit of a Benedictine and is shown with an abbot's miter and crosier. The bird refers to a legend according to which a raven saved Benedict from death by removing a piece of poisoned bread that he was about to eat.

SAN BERNARDINO
(ST BERNARDINO)

San Bernardino County, created in 1853, can boast to being the largest county in the entire United States. It derived its name from the city of San Bernardino, which itself took its name from a chapel dedicated there to Bernardino of Siena on May 20, 1810, the saint's feast day. There are also San Bernardino Mountains, a Mount San Bernardino, and a San Bernardino National Forest.

Born in Massa Marittima, near Siena, Tuscany in 1380, Bernardino was, like the inspiration for many California place names, a Franciscan friar. He was also the most celebrated preacher of his day in Italy. Covering most of the country on foot, he would draw such crowds that he had to preach outdoors, sometimes several times a day. He was known for holding up to his listeners for adoration a plaque inscribed with IHS (the first three capital letters of the Greek spelling of JESUS). Though he meant this only as a symbol for Jesus himself, the practice for a time attracted the unwelcome attentions of the Inquisition, who accused him (unsuccessfully) of idolatry. Bernardino died in 1444 while on a preaching tour.

St Bernardino of Siena. Church of San Francisco, San Miguel de Allende, Mexico.

SAN BERNARDO
(ST BERNARD)

San Bernardo Valley, in San Diego County, takes its name from a ranch named around 1800 for the medieval churchman Bernard of Clairvaux. Today there is a Rancho San Bernardo neighborhood of San Diego city. In San Luis Obispo County there is also a San Bernardo Creek.

There never actually lived any San Ardo. The rural community so named, in Monterey County, was originally called San Bernardo after a ranch of the name. The Post Office shortened this to San Ardo to avoid confusion with San Bernardino.

Born of a French aristocratic family in Burgundy around 1090, Bernard at the age of twenty-two became a monk at the monastery of Cîteaux, from which derives the name of his "Cistercian" order. He displayed such qualities of leadership there that only three years later he was appointed abbot of a new abbey at Clairvaux. From here, his influence as an administrator, theologian, and charismatic preacher so invigorated the Cistercians that by the time of his death in 1153 they had founded about four hundred establishments throughout Europe. Bernard's eloquence as a preacher earned him the name of the "Mellifluous Doctor." His brilliance had its price, however, for after his outstanding success in winning support for the Second Crusade (1147–49) this military adventure ended in complete catastrophe for its participants. The famous St Bernard dog is not named for this saint, but for St Bernard of Montjoux (*c.*923–1008).

St Bernard. Polychrome wood, eighteenth century. Iglesia Catedral Castrense de las Fuerzas Armadas, Madrid. Bernard wears the white Cistercian habit and bears an abbot's crosier and a book (symbol of his learning).

SAN BRUNO
(ST BRUNO)

Bruno, the founder of the Carthusian monastic order, ranks high among Europe's medieval monks. His name first appeared in California in today's San Mateo County in 1774 when Father Francisco Palóu applied it to a creek. Later it was extended to San Bruno Mountain and to Point San Bruno on the coast. The city of the name dates from the 1860s. There is also a San Bruno Canyon, in Santa Clara County.

Born in Cologne, Germany around 1032, Bruno was an influential lay churchman there and in Rheims, France before becoming a monk. In order to lead the contemplative life he yearned for, he with six companions obtained some land in the lonely and rugged Chartreuse massif near Grenoble, France in 1084. Here they built the monastery that eventually became the motherhouse of all later Carthusian monasteries. "Carthusian" and Charterhouse (the name for a Carthusian monastery) derive from the word Chartreuse. The Carthusians were an austere and cloistered order that became famous especially for copying manuscripts – a vital function of medieval monks for the transmission of learning before the days of printing. In his later years, Bruno was summoned to Rome as an advisor on matters of Church policy and reform. In Italy he founded another monastery, in Calabria, where he settled until his death in 1101. The celebrated green Chartreuse liqueur was originally made by the Carthusians of the Chartreuse monastery for the support of their order.

The Vision of Saint Bruno. Oil on canvas, *c.*1660, by Pier Francesco Mola. Courtesy of the J. Paul Getty Museum, Los Angeles, California.

SAN CARLOS
(ST CHARLES)

Mission San Carlos Borroméo de Carmelo, in Monterey County, properly designates what is today more generally known as Carmel Mission. The name was given perhaps in part to honor the then King of Spain, Carlos III. The second of California's missions, established by Father Serra in 1770, it originally stood in Monterey, but was moved to nearby Carmel Valley in the following year. Perhaps the prettiest of the missions in its reconstructed form, it is the burial place of Fathers Serra, Lasuén, and Crespí and was officially designated a Minor Basilica in 1961.

The city of San Carlos, in San Mateo County, was named in 1887 to commemorate an only supposedly historical occurrence (Gudde 331): It was believed that Spanish explorers first espied San Francisco Bay from a spot behind present-day San Carlos on November 4, 1769, the saint's feast day. San Carlos Pass, in Riverside County, was named by the Anza expedition in 1774. The name also occurs in San Carlos Peak, in San Benito County. Sierra County has a Saint Charles (English form) Hill.

In contrast to picturesque Carmel Mission, Charles Borroméo himself was a sixteenth-century Italian cardinal of rather stern character and countenance, as one can see from a celebrated portrait by Ambrogio Figino. Like many another high churchman of the past, he was a child of wealth and privilege, being born at his noble family's castle on Lake Maggiore in 1538. After brilliant legal studies in Milan and Pavia, he was appointed Cardinal of Milan at the age of only twenty-three. At this time he was not yet a priest (he was not ordained for another two years) — but his maternal uncle just happened to be Pope Pius IV! Nevertheless, Charles turned out a highly successful cardinal, though a conservative one who did not hesitate to employ the services of the Inquisition when he felt it necessary. However, his material concern for the victims of a famine in 1570 and for victims of the plague in Milan in 1576 attests also to his Christian charity.

St Charles. Polychrome plaster. San Carlos Cathedral (Royal Presidio Chapel), Monterey, California. (This church was originally founded as the Mission San Carlos Borroméo. It was the first stone building and is the oldest continuously functioning house of worship in California.)

SAN CARPOFORO
(ST CARPOPHORUS)

Nothing of certainty is known about the historical St Carpophorus. His existence is, however, at least preserved from oblivion in California by San Carpoforo Creek, in Monterey and San Luis Obispo Counties, named for him in the 1830s. Sometimes Carpophorus is grouped among the so-called Four Crowned Martyrs. These were four Roman soldiers (in other versions of the legend, four or even five stonemasons) who were put to death for their Christian faith under the Roman Emperor Diocletian around the year 303. In the Middle Ages they served as the patron saints of the English stonemasons' guilds.

The Four Crowned Martyrs. Marble group, 1408–13, by Nanni di Bianco. Church of Orsanmichele, Florence, Italy. Courtesy of Scala/Art Resource, NY.

SANTA CATALINA
(ST CATHERINE)

An island of great natural beauty and enchantment, Santa Catalina lies about twenty-five miles offshore from Los Angeles County. Vizcaíno named it in 1602 when his ship anchored there on the feast day of St Catherine of Alexandria (November 25). It is one of the four Catalina Islands and one of the eight Channel Islands, and the stretch of water between it and the mainland is known as the Gulf of Santa Catalina. The English form of the name appears in Saint Catherine Creek in Sierra County.

Catherine is a saint much portrayed in art – for example, by Fra Angelico, Raphael, Caravaggio, and Cranach. Nevertheless, she has now been deemed wholly legendary, and the Church suppressed her cult in 1969. Tradition has it that she was a young noblewoman of fourth-century Alexandria renowned for her beauty and intellect. As a Christian, she refused to wed the pagan Roman Emperor, who sought her hand in marriage; and she defeated in argument fifty philosophers appointed by him to refute her Christian beliefs. For this, her persecutors attempted to break her on a wheel, though unsuccessfully, as the wheel shattered. She was then beheaded with a sword. Catherine is the patron saint of students, young girls, and craftsmen who work with a wheel, such as potters and cartwrights.

Saint Catherine of Alexandria, with her wheel. Tempera colors, gold leaf, and gold paint on parchment, *c.*1469, by Taddeo Crivelli. In *Gualenghi-d'Este Hours,* courtesy of the J. Paul Getty Museum, Los Angeles, California.

SAN CAYETANO
(ST CAJETAN OR GAETANO)

San Cayetano Mountain, in Ventura County, takes its name from a Mexican land grant of 1833 and commemorates the founder of the Theatine religious order. There is also a Cayetano Creek in Napa County, and another that flows in Alameda and Contra Costa Counties.

Born in Vicenza, Italy in 1480, Cajetan was a tireless reformer within the Church around the time of the Reformation. It was in 1516, before Luther began his reforms, that he established his Theatine Order for the improvement of pastoral and lay life in an age notorious for its ecclesiastical corruption. He emphasized the importance of obedience and spirituality among the clergy, while at the same time ministering to the sick and deprived among the laity. Among his innovations was the foundation in Naples of pawnshops designed to assist the needy.

St Cajetan. Church of San José el Calvario, Cuernavaca, Mexico.

SANTA CLARA
(ST CLARE)

A personal friend of St Francis and, like him, a native of Assisi, St Clare possessed a strong appeal for California's Franciscan missionaries. Hence, it is appropriate that an early mission should have been dedicated to her: Mission Santa Clara de Asís, California's eighth mission, founded by Father Serra in 1777. Santa Clara Valley took its name from the mission, which also gave its name to the city that grew up around it. The reconstructed mission is now part of modern Santa Clara University.

To honor Clare near her feast day of August 11 in 1769, Father Crespí of the Portolá expedition named the Santa Clara Valley, in Los Angeles and Ventura Counties, after her. The Santa Clara River was then named for the valley. Santa Clarita ("little Santa Clara") River is its tributary. In the Santa Clarita Valley lies the city of Santa Clarita.

When she was only eighteen, Clare, born in 1194, renounced all her worldly possessions to become a nun under the protection of St Francis. In due course, she became the founder of her own order, the Poor Clares, dedicated, like the Franciscans, to a life of poverty, contemplation, and care of the poor and infirm. Clare spent all of her remaining days as the abbess of her convent in Assisi, where she died in 1263 and where fascinating reminders of her can be seen today. A story is told that Clare twice miraculously saved her native city from destruction when, ill, she was carried to the city walls and exposed the sacred host in a pyx or monstrance to drive off an invading army.

St Clare, with her monstrance. Wood, porcelain and fabric, 1928. On high altar of Mission Santa Clara, on the campus of Santa Clara University, Santa Clara, California.

SAN CLEMENTE
(ST CLEMENT)

On his exploratory voyage of 1602, Vizcaíno named one of today's parched Catalina Islands, in Los Angeles County, after St Clement when he stopped there to take on water around the saint's feast day of November 23. Gudde (332) finds this particularly apt in view of the fact that Clement is reported to have miraculously discovered a spring of clear water on a barren island. The city of San Clemente, in Orange County, was called after the island. The name occurs also in San Clemente Canyon, in San Diego County, and in San Clemente Creek and Ridge, in Monterey County.

Historically, Clement is noteworthy as the fourth Bishop of Rome, and hence the fourth pope. Tradition has it that he was born a Jew in Rome and was baptized by St Peter himself. For his apostolic zeal as pope, Clement was supposedly exiled by the Emperor Trajan to the Crimea, where, however, he continued his work of converting pagans and is credited with a number of miracles. Because as a Christian he opposed the worship of the Roman emperor as divine, he is said to have been martyred around the year 100 by being thrown into the sea with an anchor around his neck.

St Clement, with his anchor. Sixteenth century. Cathedral of Santa María de la Sede, Seville, Spain.

CUPERTINO

The city of Cupertino, in Santa Clara County, reminds us of the fascinating St Joseph of Copertino (different spelling), an Italian friar once celebrated for his frequent levitations. Specifically, the city takes its name from a stream (now Stevens Creek) that received the name of Joseph of Copertino from Anza in 1776.

A Franciscan, like the inspiration for many other California place names, Joseph was born into a very poor family in Copertino, southern Italy in 1603. Awkward and backward as a youth, he at first failed to gain admission into the Franciscan Order as he wished. And once he was admitted, he lived in constant friction with his superiors, who were embarrassed and alarmed by his extraordinary behavior. The reason for this was Joseph's extreme religiosity, which would send him into ecstasies during mass and at other times, too. He is also credited with having levitated on perhaps seventy different occasions. This led to his investigation by the Inquisition, though he was, fortunately, found innocent of heresy or witchcraft. Nevertheless, Joseph the "Flying Friar," as he has been called, was secluded for the last thirty-five to forty years of his life, dying at his monastery in Osimo in 1663.

St Joseph of Cupertino, in the act of levitating. Church of Santa Maria della Stella, in the Umbrian countryside near Todi, Italy.

SAN DIEGO
(ST DIDACUS)

San Diego does not, as is sometimes thought, represent a variant spelling of Santiago (St James), but refers to the Spanish St Didacus of Alcalá. San Diego Bay had first been discovered and named San Miguel by Cabrillo in 1542. It was renamed by Vizcaíno in 1602, however, when his flagship, the *San Didacus*, anchored there around the saint's feast day of November 12. The earliest map to show the modern spelling San Diego appeared in Amsterdam in 1624 (Gudde 332–333). Alta California's first presidio and earliest Spanish community were founded here in 1769, and Father Serra founded his Mission San Diego de Alcalá nearby in the same year. Moved a few miles to its present site in 1774, this "Mother of the Missions" was designated a Minor Basilica in 1976. San Dieguito ("little San Diego") occurs in various names in San Diego County also.

Didacus illustrates the connection between humility and sanctity in the Christian tradition. He was born of a poor family in San Nicolás del Puerto, Spain in 1400 and, after living as a recluse for a time, joined the Franciscans as a lay brother while still a young man. He first worked as a missionary in the Canary Islands for a few years, and then spent the rest of his life in various Spanish friaries, finally in Alcalá (near Madrid), where he died in 1463. Officially, he performed only routine chores, such as guarding the door or cooking, yet he achieved fame during his lifetime for his holiness, his charities, and his reputed healing powers.

St Didacus, distributing food to the poor. Church of San Francisco, Santiago de Compostela, Spain.

SAN DIMAS
(ST DISMAS)

The initial settlement at San Dimas, Los Angeles County, was known as Mud Springs, which eager land developers presumably found unlikely to attract new customers when a railroad opened through the area in 1887. Hence the appellation was changed to echo nearby San Dimas Canyon, named in the early nineteenth century by a settler originally from San Dimas in northern Mexico. Local historian Nicholas Polos, according to the city's website, has shown there is no truth to the tale that San Dimas took its name from Dismas, the Biblical repentant thief, because bandits once frequented the area.

Dismas (from the Greek word meaning "dying") is the name traditionally given to the Good Thief crucified beside Jesus. We read of the exchange between them in Luke 23: 39–43, where Dismas begs Jesus, "Lord, remember me when you come into your kingdom." To this, Jesus replies, "Today you will be with me in Paradise." Dismas is shown in art with his eyes raised to heaven and on Jesus's right. He has traditionally been venerated as the patron saint of prisoners and thieves.

St Dismas. Polychrome wood. Church of Nuestra
Señora de la Asunción (Ex Convento de la Natividad), Tepoztlan, Mexico.

MISSION DOLORES

Mission Dolores is the name generally used today for San Francisco Mission. It originally stood near a lake fed by a stream named by Anza in 1776 in honor of Nuestra Señora de los Dolores (Our Lady of the Sorrows) on the last Friday of Lent, which at that time was her feast day. This designation of the Virgin recalls what tradition terms the Seven Sorrows of the Virgin: Jesus's circumcision; the flight into Egypt; Jesus lost in the temple; the meeting with Jesus on his way to Calvary; the crucifixion; the descent from the cross; and the entombment.

Our Lady of the Sorrows. Polychrome wood bust, seventeenth century, from the school of Gregorio Fernandez. Church of San Juan, Alba de Tormes, Spain. The seven swords in Mary's breast represent her seven sorrows.

SAN DOMINGO
(ST DOMINIC)

St Dominic (properly, Santo Domingo in Spanish) was the founder of the Dominican Order of monks, which in the past was not infrequently a rival of the Franciscans in the Americas as well as in Europe. Perhaps for that reason, relatively few features are named for Dominic, or other Dominicans, in California. There are, however, San Domingo Creeks in Calaveras and Sacramento Counties.

Born in Spain around 1170, Dominic de Guzmán was, in fact, a contemporary of St Francis. In contrast to him, however, the motive force in Dominic's life was the resolve to combat the divisive forces (subsumable under the term "heresy") that in his lifetime threatened to rend the Church. In particular, his efforts were directed against the so-called Albigensian heretics in France. His order, officially called the Order of Preachers, was founded in 1215 and was dedicated to scholarship, teaching, and above all preaching. Some of the greatest scholars of the medieval Church, such as Sts Albert the Great and Thomas Aquinas were Dominicans. Dominic died in Italy in 1221, shortly before the establishment of the Inquisition, which, directed at the outset largely by Dominicans, combated heresies, real or imaginary.

St Dominic (left). Polychrome ceramic, 1920s, by Dal Prato Statuary. Sts Peter and Paul Church, San Francisco, California. This interesting group shows Dominic and St Catherine of Siena with the Virgin and Child. Dominic holds a rosary because he is said (traditionally, but unhistorically) to have originated the devotion to the rosary. A dog with a flaming torch in its jaws accompanies him, an emblematical reference to the image of Dominic as the Lord's watchdog who would bring truth and light to the world. The group is based on a celebrated painting, by an unknown artist, in the Shrine of Our Lady of the Rosary, in Pompeii, Italy.

SAN ELIJO
(ST ALEXIS OR ALEXIUS)

In 1769 the Portolá expedition gave the name of San Alejo to a spot where they camped on July 16, the day before the feast day of St Alexis, a probably legendary, or (depending on the source one consults) perhaps fifth-century, Roman saint. The place was near today's San Elijo Valley and Lagoon, in San Diego County, the name having changed spelling, Gudde (333) suggests, due to confusion between Alejo and a St Eligio (Eligius or Eloi). There is also a planned community of San Elijo Hills in San Diego County.

The story goes that the young Alexis had sworn to dedicate himself to God, but nevertheless married because his parents had arranged a match for him. With the assent of his wife, however, he left her on their wedding night in order to undertake a pilgrimage to the Holy Land. On his return home, he lived for seventeen years as a beggar, unrecognized, under the stairs of his father's residence in Rome. He was identified only on his death by a letter in his possession written in his own hand, by miracles, and by heavenly voices. This story made Alexis a patron saint of beggars, pilgrims, and travelers.

The Discovery of the Body of Saint Alexis, Oil on canvas, c.1640s,
by Étienne de La Tour. Alexis holds the letter that helped identify him. Previously attributed to Georges de La Tour, the painting is a copy of a lost original. Courtesy of The National Gallery of Ireland, Dublin.

SAINT ELMO
(ALSO KNOWN AS ST ERASMUS IN ENGLISH)

The name Saint (English form) Elmo occurs in Saint Elmo Creek, in Sonoma County, and in the locality of Saint Elmo, in San Bernardino County. Like many another saint, Elmo is better known in legend than in history. He was in truth a bishop of Formiae, Italy who was martyred for his faith around 303 during the Emperor Diocletian's persecutions. Legend has elaborated this bare fact, however, by expanding on his cruel tortures, which include having his intestines extracted by a windlass, as one can see in the accompanying illustration.

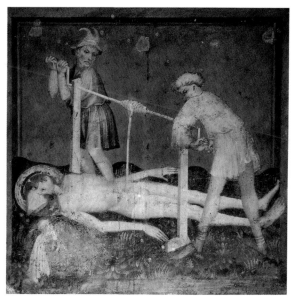

The Martyrdom of St Elmo. On a stone pillar, *c.*1450, attributed to Erasmus Schüchlin. Ulm Cathedral, Germany.

SAN EMIGDIO
(ST EMIGDIUS OR EMYDIUS)

A saint traditionally invoked for protection against earthquakes, Emigdius has appropriately given his name to some features in Kern County, a seismically active area. The county's San Emigdio Canyon, Creek, and Mountains were called after a San Emigdio ranch of Mission Santa Barbara, recorded since 1823. There is also a San Emigdio Blue butterfly (*Plebeius emigdionis*), native to southern California.

Emigdius's life story is somewhat confused, as the sources contradict each other. It appears, however, that he was born around 250 in

Trier, now in Germany but at that time a Roman city. He became Bishop of the city of Ascoli in Italy, but was beheaded by the Roman authorities as a Christian in 303. His connection with earthquakes dates from only 1703. In this year an earthquake destroyed many towns and villages in central Italy, but spared Ascoli, a circumstance attributed to Emigdius, who was, and still is, the city's patron saint. Interestingly, St Emydius's church in San Francisco received its name because so many of its original parishioners were refugees from the 1906 San Francisco earthquake.

St Emigdius. Mosaic, 2006, by Judson Studios (Los Angeles). Church of St Emydius, Lynwood, California.

SANTA FE
(ST FAITH)

One might be excused for assuming that St Faith is simply an allegory for the Christian faith. In fact, however, this saint is more than an abstraction, as she combines allegory with historical fact and with legend. There did indeed live a young Christian girl of the name (French: Foy) who was martyred by the Romans in Agen, in south central France sometime in the third century. Her relics were taken to the nearby town of Conques, where they are preserved today in a splendid reliquary in the abbey church. As is often the case, the life of this virtually unknown girl was embroidered by legend, according to which she was roasted on a brazier before being beheaded. In earlier days she was widely venerated in England, Spain, and Italy, as well as in France.

In the United States, St Faith's name has been made famous by the Santa Fe Railway and by the New Mexico city of Santa Fe. In California, the name occurs in the town of Santa Fe Springs in Los Angeles County, in the San Diego community of Rancho Santa Fe, and in Santa Fe Channel in Contra Costa County.

St Faith. Wooden reliquary with gilded silver, copper, enamel, rock crystal and precious stones, ninth century with Gothic additions. Abbey Ste Foy, Conques, France. Courtesy of Erich Lessing/Art Resource, NY.

SAN FELIPE
(ST PHILIP)

The Apostle Philip has given his name to localities in Santa Clara and San Diego Counties, as well as to a number of natural features in these counties and in San Benito and Imperial Counties.

Philip was one of Jesus's earliest disciples and is mentioned in the Bible specifically at the Feeding of the Five Thousand. After the crucifixion, nothing of certainty is known about his activities. Early Christian tradition claims, however, that he preached the gospel in Phrygia, in Asia Minor, and that he was also martyred there by being crucified.

St Philip. Marble, 1703–12, by Giuseppe Mazzuoli.
Basilica of St John Lateran, Rome.

SAN FERNANDO
(ST FERDINAND)

Ferdinand was a saint undoubtedly dear to the hearts of California's missionaries. He was not only a Spanish king, but also a Franciscan tertiary (lay affiliate of the order), and was, too, the patron of San Fernando College in Mexico City, where missionaries destined for California received their training. Father Lasuén dedicated Mission San Fernando Rey de España (King of Spain), in present-day Los Angeles County, to him in 1797. The seventeenth of California's missions, it subsequently gave its name to the San Fernando Valley and the city of San Fernando.

St Ferdinand. Polychrome wood altar statue, sent from Mexico in 1808. With kind permission of Mission San Fernando Rey, Mission Hills, California.

Through inheritance, Ferdinand III (1199–1252) united under him the previously independent realms of León and Castile, so creating as his kingdom a major part of what today is Spain. Beyond that, he enlarged his territories through war, defeating the Moors and recapturing from them for Christian Spain the greater part of Andalusia in the south of the country. His rule was comparatively benign and enlightened, however, as both Muslims and Jews enjoyed religious tolerance under him – a tolerance rescinded by the later Catholic monarchs Ferdinand and Isabella in 1492. Another sign of Ferdinand III's general progressiveness was his enlargement of the University of Salamanca, making it one of Europe's leading seats of learning.

SAN FRANCISCO
(ST FRANCIS)

San Francisco is a name especially resonant in California, not only because of the beauty, culture, and excitement of the city that bears it, but because it refers to the patron saint of the fathers who built the California missions. San Francisco Bay was discovered for Spain by a detachment of Portolá's expedition in 1769, though the name was not formally applied to it until after 1775. Father Francisco Palóu founded Mission San Francisco (see **Mission Dolores**) in 1776 as the sixth of California's twenty-one. The presidio (the third of California's four) was founded in the same year. A village at Yerba Buena Cove on the bay,

St Francis. Detail of mural, 1920, by Luigi Brusatori. National Shrine of St Francis of Assisi, San Francisco, California.

established in 1835, became the city named San Francisco in 1847, while San Francisco County (one the state's original twenty-seven) was created in 1850.

The name San Francisquito ("little San Francisco") is applied to various features in San Mateo, Santa Clara, Monterey, and Los Angeles Counties.

Francis is one of the best loved of all Christian saints, for with his emphasis on simplicity, modesty, charity, and love of nature he epitomizes, for many, values often under siege in our age, and perhaps in any age. He was born in Assisi, Umbria in 1181, and after a religious conversion in his youth abandoned the comforts of his wealthy merchant-class home for a life of poverty, labor, contemplation, and dedication to God and the service of others. He was, however, at the same time also an ecstatic and a mystic who in 1224 received the first recorded stigmata – the signs of the wounds Jesus had received to his hands, feet, and side. Attracting many followers to him, he received approval in 1210 for the monastic order that was named for him the Order of St Francis. He died in 1226 and is entombed in the beautiful, but rather inappropriately ornate, Basilica of St Francis in Assisi. Many great artists, including Giotto, Fra Angelico, Gozzoli, Bellini, Caravaggio, and Jan van Eyck, have depicted Francis or scenes from his life. On a more mundane level, garden statuary often shows him in the characteristic pose of feeding the birds and animals.

San Francisco Solano.

SAN FRANCISCO SOLANO
(ST FRANCIS SOLANO)

Mission San Francisco Solano was dedicated to a Spanish Franciscan revered by the California missionaries for his work among the South American Indians. Father José Altimira founded it in 1823 as the twenty-first, last, and most northerly of California's missions. It stands in Sonoma, in Solano County, and was the only mission created during the Mexican era in California. On the plaza adjacent to the mission was raised the Bear Flag, marking the inception of the short-lived (four-week) Republic of California in 1846 and heralding the conquest of the region by the United States in the Mexican-American War.

Born near Córdoba in 1549, Francis already enjoyed a reputation as an eloquent preacher before being sent to South America as a missionary in 1589. For twenty years he then traveled far and wide through Argentina, Chile, Paraguay, Colombia, and especially Peru. He converted many of the native people to Christianity, but was also zealous in his opposition to abuses of the clergy and of the Spanish ruling class. Dying in Lima, Peru in 1610, he has been called the "Apostle of the Americas."

St Francis Solano. Oil on canvas. With kind permission of Mission San Francisco Solano, Sonoma, California.

SAN GABRIEL
(ST GABRIEL)

The name of Gabriel the Archangel is attached to a number of major sites in Los Angeles County. It was first applied by Portolá in 1769 to the San Gabriel Valley, and was later extended to the mission, river, mountains, peak, and city. In 1771 Fathers Cambón and Somera founded Mission San Gabriel Arcángel, the fourth of California's twenty-one and known as the "Pride of the Missions." It was of vital importance for the supply and support of Spanish overland expeditions from Sonora in northwestern Mexico to the California coastal missions and presidios.

With Michael and Raphael, Gabriel is one of the archangels mentioned in the Bible. As such, he was not a person of flesh and blood, but rather a spiritual entity. His most important appearance in scripture is at the Annunciation, when he makes known to Mary that she will bear God's son (Luke 1: 26–38). In *Paradise Lost*, Milton portrays him as one of the leaders of the Hosts of Heaven. Somewhat quaintly, because of his role of ethereal messenger, Gabriel has been declared the patron saint of telecommunications workers.

St Gabriel, with Mary. *The Annunciation.* Distemper on linen, *c.*1450–55, by Dieric Bouts. Courtesy of the J. Paul Getty Museum, Los Angeles, California.

SAINT GEORGE

The English form of Point Saint George, in Del Norte County, reveals the fact that the Spanish did not name it. It was, in fact, so called by the British navigator George Vancouver in the course of his historic charting of the west coast of North America from California to Alaska. He gave it the name on April 23, 1792, the feast day of St George, the patron saint of England and of Vancouver himself. There are also a nearby Saint George Reef and Channel.

George is, of course, a familiar saint, for who is unacquainted with him as the mounted dragon slayer? He has been portrayed as such by artists like Bellini, Uccello, Carpaccio, Raphael, and Dürer. Yet George was more real than his mythical dragon might lead one to suspect. There did indeed live a historical George, who was probably a Roman soldier in Asia Minor, martyred for his faith sometime in the early fourth century. Around this figure a clearly legendary tale has grown. The George of legend is a Christian knight on horseback rescuing a princess (symbol of the Church) from the power of a fearsome dragon (symbol of evil). This saint is the patron of soldiers, of boy scouts, and of various countries, including England and Portugal.

Saint George and the Dragon. Illumination, *c.*1471, by Lieven van Lathem, in *Prayer Book of Charles the Bold.* Courtesy of the J. Paul Getty Museum, Los Angeles, California.

SAN GERONIMO
(ST JEROME)

Though a towering figure in early Church history, St Jerome put in a rather late appearance in California. His name first occurs in a Mexican land grant in today's Marin County in 1844. The land grant subsequently gave its name to present-day San Geronimo Creek, Valley, and community.

Born around 341 in Stridon, in what is today Croatia, Jerome is celebrated for his translation into Latin of the original Hebrew and Greek scriptures of the Old and New Testaments. Known as the Vulgate, this became the standard version of the Bible used at first in all Christian churches, and after the Reformation in all Catholic churches. It remained the standard Latin Bible until 1979.

Part of Jerome's life was spent in the area of the eastern Mediterranean, where he lived for five years as a hermit in the Syrian wilderness and where he is supposed to have befriended a lion by removing a thorn from its paw. For a time he also resided, and indeed died (in 420), in Jerusalem. Here the Roman matron Paula, who was later canonized and has provided the name for the Ventura County town of Santa Paula, supported him in his scholarly work on the Bible. Otherwise Jerome lived in Rome, where he served as personal assistant to Pope Damasus, for which reason (though unhistorically) he is often depicted in art with a cardinal's hat, as in works by Botticelli, Ghirlandaio, Bellini, Crivelli, Caravaggio, Dürer, and Bosch. For his erudition, Jerome was declared one of the Latin Doctors of the Church.

Saint Jerome in the Wilderness. Tempera on panel, *c.*1470, by Ercole de'Roberti. One can see both Jerome's lion and his cardinal's hat in this painting. Courtesy of the J. Paul Getty Museum, Los Angeles, California.

SANTA GERTRUDIS
(ST GERTRUDE)

St Gertrude, a German Benedictine nun, was one of the most notable visionaries and mystics of her age. Born in 1256, she lived from the time of her education as a young girl until her death in 1302 entirely in her convent in Helfta, Thuringia. Her writings include prayers and reflections on the scriptures and on Church liturgy. Though histories refer to her as "the Great," Gertrude's fame has sadly faded today. Her name lives on, however, in Santa Gertrudis Creek, in Riverside County, first recorded in 1821.

St Gertrude. Polychrome wood. With kind permission of Mission San Buenaventura, Ventura, California.

SAN GORGONIO
(ST GORGONIUS)

Though an unfamiliar saint's name nowadays, Gorgonius is recalled by a number of major sites in Riverside County. Occurring first in 1824 in a ranch of Mission San Gabriel, the name San Gorgonio was later applied to San Gorgonio Pass and to nearby San Gorgonio Wilderness, Creek, and Mountain (sometimes known as Grayback).

Perhaps, as Wagner (55) suggests, the name commemorates that saint sometimes known as Gorgonius of Rome. Born in the imperial city, he was for a time a trusted retainer at the court of Diocletian, an emperor notorious for his persecution of Christians. Discovering that his servant had converted to Christianity, Diocletian had him executed together with several others in 303. This Gorgonius, however, is frequently confused and conflated with another saint of the same name, who was martyred (probably also in 303) as a Christian in the city of Nicomedia, in Asia Minor. Gorgonius of Nicomedia may be shown with one or the other of his companions, Peter and Dorotheus, who were executed together with him.

The Martyrdom of Sts Gorgonius and Dorotheus. From *Vie des saints*, fourteenth century, by Richard de Montbaston and others.

79

SAN GREGORIO
(ST GREGORY)

The medieval Pope Gregory the Great, one of the most influential popes of all time, has served as the inspiration for several place names in San Mateo County. The community of San Gregorio takes its name from a Mexican land grant of 1839, while the name is applied also to a creek, beach, valley, and mountain.

Born of a patrician family in Rome around 540, Gregory spent much of his inherited wealth on the building of monasteries after he became a monk at the age of thirty-three. When fifty, he was elected pope. A man

of energy and intellect, he did much to centralize and strengthen the power of the papacy. He also codified the church music of his day, in recognition of which the Gregorian Chant is named for him. His writings include Lives of the Saints and letters. For his scholarship, Gregory enjoys the title of Latin Doctor of the Church. He is also known as the "Apostle of the English" because it was he who in 596 sent missionaries to Christianize the Anglo-Saxons of southern England.

St Gregory. Stained glass. Church of St Monica, San Francisco, California. The dove symbolizes Gregory's inspiration by the Holy Spirit.

SAN GUILLERMO
(ST WILLIAM)

There lived several St Williams, and it is unknown which of these is commemorated in San Guillermo Creek and Mountain, Ventura County. Certainly, however, the name goes back to Spanish times.

Probably the best-known Williams are William of Aquitaine and William of Maleval, who share certain characteristics. Both were French, and both were soldiers before withdrawing from the world. Duke William of Aquitaine was, indeed, considered the very model of a Christian knight. He was one of Charlemagne's commanders against the Moors before becoming a monk in 806 — a story that provided the subject matter for the thirteenth-century German epic poem *Willehalm*. His namesake, William of Maleval, was a dissolute soldier prior to settling as a hermit near Siena, Tuscany around the middle of the twelfth century.

St William, the soldier. Marble, 1690.
St Stephen's Cathedral, Vienna.

SAINT HELENA
(ST HELEN)

A tale more charming than true relates that Mount Saint Helena, in Sonoma County, received its name from a Russian princess called Helena who planted the Russian flag atop its peak in 1841 in honor of her patron saint. Most probably, however, it was so named by the colonists of the Russian settlement at Fort Ross (1812–41) to commemorate the visit of the Russian ship *Saint Helena* to California in 1841. The city of Saint Helena, in the heart of California's wine-producing Napa Valley, was named in 1855.

Helen is a notable figure in the history of the Church. Though born an innkeeper's daughter in the Roman province of Bithynia, in Asia Minor, around 220, she became through her marriage to a Roman general the mother of the future Roman Emperor Constantine. It was Constantine who in 313 first declared religious freedom for Christians throughout the Empire. Converting to Christianity rather late in life, Helen spent her last years in the Holy Land. Here, it is claimed, she helped unearth the cross on which Jesus died. Subsequently parts of this cross and its nails, and pieces of wood or metal that had touched the cross, were peddled throughout Europe as holy relics. This is the "Holy Cross" that gave its name to Mission Santa Cruz, founded by Father Lasuén in 1791.

St Helen, with her holy cross. Polychrome wood, nineteenth century.
Church of San Agustín, Morelia, Mexico.

SAN IGNACIO
(ST IGNATIUS)

San Ignacio is a tiny community with a big name. Located in eastern San Diego County within Los Coyotes Indian Reservation, it recalls St Ignatius Loyola, an outstanding figure in Church history.

A Spaniard like so many of California's saints, Ignatius was born in his noble family's Castle of Loyola in 1491. He served as a professional soldier until, immobilized by a battle wound, he underwent a religious conversion at the age of thirty. After making a pilgrimage to Jerusalem, he studied at various universities, latterly at the University of Paris. Here he gathered about him a group of young men who subsequently formed the nucleus of his Society of Jesus (Jesuits). The purpose of the Jesuit order, approved in 1540, was to counteract the Protestant Reformation in Europe and to spread the Catholic faith abroad, in Asia and the Americas. Ignatius was the order's founder and first General from its inception until his death in Rome in 1556. The Jesuits became one of the Church's foremost teaching and missionary orders and established famous schools and universities in many lands. Though in the past censured for their sometimes sinister ways (resulting in their official disbandment by the Church in the years 1773 to 1814), they have also been, and continue to be, staunch defenders of the downtrodden in many of the least fortunate corners of the globe.

St Ignatius of Loyola. Bronze statue, 2002, by Lisa Reinertson.
Santa Clara University, Santa Clara, California.

SAN JACINTO
(ST HYACINTH)

The saint with the charming appellation of Hyacinth in English is commemorated in a considerable number of California locations. The name was first used in 1821 when Mission San Luis Rey established a ranch that they named San Jacinto. It was then extended to a river, valley, lake, mountain, mountains, basin, fault, and Indian Reservation, as well as to the city of San Jacinto, all in Riverside County.

Born the scion of a noble family in Poland in 1185, Hyacinth (Polish: Iazech) experienced a sudden conversion to religion when he met St Dominic on a visit to Rome in 1220. Becoming a Dominican himself, he returned to Poland, where his brilliance as a preacher advanced the interests of his order in that country. He was instrumental in founding no fewer than five Polish Dominican monasteries, from which missionaries went out to evangelize distant parts of eastern Europe and Scandinavia. Dying in 1257, he is entombed in the Dominican church of Krakow, Poland, and is a patron of Poland.

St Hyacinth. Stained glass, 1955, by Harold W. Cummings Studios (San Francisco). Chapel of the Dominican Sisters at Mission San Jose, Fremont, California. The saint holds a monstrance and a statue of the Virgin and Child. Tradition relates that he rescued such objects from a monastery that was under attack.

SAINT JAMES

The English navigator Francis Drake originally named today's Farallon Islands (just outside the Golden Gate) after St James in 1579 when he stopped there for two days, on July 24 and 25 (St James's Day), in the course of his epic circumnavigation of the globe. The Isle of Saint James (actually a group of three islets and assorted rocks in the Farallons) still bears the name. Ironically, James is the patron saint of Spain, whose ships and cities Drake raided in the Americas and whose naval forces he successfully evaded by sailing up the coast of California.

Sometimes called "the Great," St James was the brother of John the Apostle and was one of the foremost among Jesus's disciples. With Peter and John he was one of the witnesses of Jesus's transfiguration and of the Agony in the Garden. After the crucifixion, he was the first of the disciples to be martyred by being put to the sword in Jerusalem in the year 44.

James's links with Spain are numerous, but largely legendary, and there is little likelihood that he either preached or died in that country. The Cathedral of Santiago de Compostela in northwest Spain claims his relics, however. This made Compostela, after Rome and Jerusalem, the most important pilgrimage destination for all of medieval Europe. Even today it continues to draw great numbers of pilgrims, many on foot. Legend claims that James appeared mounted on a white charger to lead the Christian Spaniards to victory over the Moors at the Battle of Clavijo in 844. For this reason he is sometimes portrayed as Santiago Matamoros (St James Slayer of the Moors), as in paintings by Tiepolo and Juan Carreño de Miranda.

Santiago Matamoros. This Slayer of the Moors charges out of the gloom of a side chapel in the Cathedral of Santiago de Compostela, Spain.

SAN JOAQUIN
(ST JOACHIM)

Given the prominence of Santa Ana among California place names, it is little wonder that Anne's husband, Joachim (Spanish: Joaquín), should have been likewise honored. The San Joaquin River, one of the state's major waterways, was so named by Lieutenant Gabriel Moraga in 1805 or 1806, and by about 1854 the name was extended to the entire southern part of the great Central Valley. San Joaquin County, one of California's original twenty-seven, was created in 1850. A post office in Fresno County received the name in the 1880s, and around it grew today's city of San Joaquin. There are also San Joaquin Hills, in Orange County, and a San Joaquin Peak, in San Benito County.

As the husband of the Virgin Mary's mother, Joachim is frequently shown in Anne's company in art – for instance, in works by Giotto, Gozzoli, Signorelli, and Dürer. Nothing of historical certainty is known about either of the two saints, however. According to the second-century apocryphal gospel of James, Joachim was suspect in the eyes of his fellow Jews because his long marriage to Anne had remained childless. In their old age, however, an angel appeared to the couple announcing that a child would be born to them. Joachim is a patron saint of fathers and grandfathers.

St Joachim. Polychrome wood, Mexican. With kind permission of Mission San Jose, Fremont, California. As in the Mexican tradition, the elderly Joachim here leans on a stick and wears a robe bordered with ermine.

SAINT JOHN

If one follows Gudde (327), Saint John as a California place designation generally derives from a modern person's name. This is the case with Mount Saint John, in Glenn County, named for A. C. St John, a settler of the early 1850s. Similarly, Saint Johns River, in Tulare County, was named for a Loomis St John. Saint John Mountain, in Napa County, was probably called for a local person when so named in the 1890s, while Saint John occurs also in the name of a canyon in Mendocino County.

St John the Apostle (or the Evangelist) is characterized in the Bible as the "disciple whom Jesus loved." As such, he is portrayed next to Jesus in pictures of the Last Supper. He is often shown in art as youthful, beardless, and longhaired, so that he may sometimes appear almost feminine. (This circumstance becomes pivotal for the plot of Dan Brown's best-selling novel *The DaVinci Code* of 2003.) The fourth gospel is normally attributed to him, though there is no firm evidence that the historical John composed either it or the Book of Revelation, also frequently credited to him. After the crucifixion, he traveled throughout much of the Mediterranean region preaching the word. He is reputedly the only disciple not to have been martyred, as he is said to have died at an old age in Ephesus, Greece. Because of the sublime style of his gospel, John's emblem in art is an eagle.

St John the Evangelist. Oil on canvas, 1625–28, by Franz Hals. John's eagle looks over his shoulder. Courtesy of the J. Paul Getty Museum, Los Angeles, California.

SAN JOSE
(ST JOSEPH)

Founded in 1777 as a secular settlement by José Joaquín Moraga (second-in-command of the 1775–76 Anza expedition), the city of San Jose (Spanish: José) can boast to being the state's oldest civic municipality, as well as its first capital (from 1849 to 1851). Unusually for California, then, the city predates the mission, which was established in 1797 by Father Lasuén as California's fourteenth. Mission San Jose stands today not in the city of San Jose, but in Fremont, Alameda County. The saint has given his name to many other geographical features in California, too, for instance, in San Diego, Los Angeles, Marin, Santa Barbara, and Monterey Counties.

Joseph was the husband of the Virgin Mary, whom he married though she was already pregnant with God's son, after he had been so informed by an angel. Though he was himself a carpenter of Nazareth, he was, as the gospel of Matthew relates, descended from the line of the Jewish King David. Joseph is regarded as a model father and husband, and as such is the patron saint of families. He is also the patron of workers and of the entire Church.

St Joseph, with the Child Jesus. Stained glass. Church of the Immaculate Conception, San Diego (Old Town), California.

SAN JUAN BAUTISTA
(ST JOHN THE BAPTIST)

John the Baptist, one of the best known Biblical saints, gave his name to Mission San Juan Bautista, in San Benito County, founded in 1797 by Father Fermín de Lasuén on St John's feast day of June 24. It was the fifteenth of California's missions and one of the largest, with a church able to accommodate a thousand people. Today's attractive little city, adjacent to and named for the mission, was begun in 1814.

John the Baptist, just a little older than Jesus, is said in Luke's gospel to have been Jesus's kinsman. A wilderness-dwelling prophet, he attracted a considerable band of followers, including the later Christian apostles Andrew, Peter, and James. He recognized Jesus as the Messiah, however, when he baptized him in the River Jordan – hence his appellation "the Baptist."

John made an enemy of King Herod of Judea by vilifying him and his Queen Herodias as incestuous because Herodias was Herod's niece and his brother's widow. For this reason, Salome, Herodias's daughter, danced to please Herod so that she might receive a boon from him – namely, John the Baptist's head. Salome dancing or with the Baptist's severed head is a frequent subject in art – for instance, in works by Caravaggio, Cranach, Dolci, Gozzoli, Guido Reni, and Aubrey Beardsley. John also figures prominently in Richard Strauss's opera *Salome* of 1905.

St John the Baptist. Bronze, 2000, by Thomas Marsh. Mission San Juan Bautista, San Juan Bautista, California.

St John of Capistrano. Oil on canvas. With kind permission of Mission San Juan Capistrano, San Juan Capistrano, California.

SAN JUAN CAPISTRANO
(ST JOHN OF CAPISTRANO)

Known as the "Jewel of the California Missions," Mission San Juan Capistrano, in Orange County, was founded by Father Serra in 1776 as the seventh of California's twenty-one. Mostly a romantic ruin today, set in an attractive garden, it is popularly famed for its swallows, which are said to depart each year on October 23, the saint's feast day, and to return on March 19. This is commemorated in Leon René's song of 1938, "When the swallows come back to Capistrano." The settlement that grew up around the mission was incorporated as a city in 1961.

As his name suggests, John was born in Capistrano, Italy (in 1386). Though married for a time, he separated from his wife in order to become a Franciscan at the age of thirty. He soon made a name for himself as a fiery preacher, though not always in a capacity one might admire today. He became a zealous Inquisitor-General for Vienna in the 1450s, for instance, and in 1453 preached a crusade against the Turks. He is remembered for the part he played in the defeat of the Turks at the Battle of Belgrade in 1456, in which year he also died.

NORTH SAN JUAN

The remote little village of North San Juan, in Nevada County, goes back to a German miner who discovered gold in the area in 1853. He called the nearby hill San Juan Hill because it reminded him of the prominence on which stands the prison of San Juan de Ulloa that he had seen in Vera Cruz during the Mexican-American War. When a post office was opened there in 1857, North was added to the place name to distinguish it from California's other San Juans.

KINGS RIVER AND CANYON

In 1805 the explorer Lieutenant Gabriel Moraga was the first European to enter the area of Kings River. He named it the Río de los Santos Reyes (River of the Holy Kings), the day being Epiphany (January 6), the day on which the Three Kings arrived to worship the baby Jesus. Kings County was created in 1893, and Kings Canyon National Park in 1940.

The story of the Magi, or wise men, from the East who followed a star to find the Christ Child in his manger is familiar from Matthew's gospel (2: 1–12). After they had presented the infant with their gifts of gold, myrrh, and frankincense, they returned home without reporting their find to King Herod, in accordance with a command they had received from an angel. Tradition has made kings of the Magi and given them the names Balthazar, Casper, and Melchior. They are revered as saints.

The Meeting of the Three Kings, with David and Isaiah. Oil and gold leaf on panel, before 1480, by the Master of the St. Bartholomew Altarpiece. Courtesy of the J. Paul Getty Museum, Los Angeles, California.

SAN LEANDRO
(ST LEANDER)

San Leandro Creek, in Alameda County, was so named in 1828 for the Spanish bishop St Leander of Seville. The city of San Leandro was laid out in 1855, while there are also San Leandro Hills, as well as a Bay and Reservoir, all in Alameda County.

Leander was Bishop of Seville from 584 until his death in 600. In this capacity he was an upholder of Christian orthodoxy and worked hard for the conversion of heretics – a task that might win him little praise in our own more ecumenical times, but which has to be understood in the context of his less tolerant age. Leander supervised the education of his younger brother Isidore (Spanish: Ysidro), who became Bishop of Sevill after him (600–630), was one of the most learned men in the Europe of his day, and was also · canonized. According to Gudde (350–350), San Ysidro as a California place name probably derives not from this Isidore the Bishop, however, but from Isidore the Farmer.

Sts Leander and Isidore. Oil on canvas, 1655, by Bartolomé Esteban Murillo. Museum of Seville Cathedral, Spain. Leander is on the left, and the scholar Isidore, with book and pen, is on the right.

SAN LORENZO
(ST LAURENCE)

It is hardly surprising that Laurence, as one of the most notable early Roman martyrs, should be commemorated in California. The name San Lorenzo occurs as early as 1769 when the Portolá expedition applied it to the San Lorenzo River, in present-day Santa Cruz County. The community of San Lorenzo, in Alameda County, was laid out in 1854, though the name was used in the area probably as early as 1812. There is also a San Lorenzo Creek, in Monterey County.

A native of Spain, Laurence was the deacon and almsgiver of the third-century Pope Sixtus II in a period when the Christian Church still suffered persecution from Roman imperial authorities. After the pope himself was put to death on the orders of Emperor Valerian, Laurence was commanded to surrender the Church's treasure to the state. When he refused to comply and instead pointed to Rome's poor as the "Church's treasure," he was put to death in 258, most likely by the sword. Legend claims, however, that he was roasted alive on an iron grill and that he told his tormentors to turn him over when his first side was cooked through. For this reason, he is the patron saint of cooks today!

St Laurence, with his iron grill. Basilica of San Lorenzo fuori le Mura, Rome.

LOS ANGELES

Los Angeles, the largest city in the state, should rightly be included in this book as its name refers, in its original full form, to Our Lady. Portolá's expedition camped on August 2, 1769 by a stream that they named for Nuestra Señora la Reina de los Ángeles de la Portiúncula (Our Lady the Queen of the Angels of the Portiuncula), whose feast they had celebrated the previous day. The name alludes to the little chapel of the Portiuncula (now enclosed within the Basilica of Our Lady of the Angels) near Assisi that was closely associated with the historical St

(Our Lady of the Angels.) The Assumption of the Virgin. Oil and gold leaf on panel, before 1480, by the Master of the St Bartholomew Altarpiece. Courtesy of the J. Paul Getty Museum, Los Angeles, California.

Francis. In 1781 a town was begun called El Pueblo de Nuestra Señora la Reina de los Ángeles, which became popularly known as the Pueblo de Los Ángeles. As such, it was, after San Jose, California's second town with secular government. The city of Los Angeles was incorporated in 1850, in the same year as the county was organized.

Among Our Lady's various appellations, Our Lady "of the Angels" is one of the more prominent. In this guise she is shown in art in the company of angels praising her or furthering her work.

Angel Island in San Francisco Bay was originally named the Isla de los Ángeles by Captain Juan Ayala in 1775. He anchored there on the feast day of Our Lady of the Angels during the first systematic survey of the Bay.

SAINT LOUIS

Gudde (327) reports that settlers from St Louis in Missouri probably named the community of Saint Louis, in Sierra County, and Saint Louis Mountain, in Sonoma County. If this is so, the Louis referred to was the sainted King Louis IX of France, the Missouri city having been founded by French settlers in what was at the time French North America. (See also under **San Luis Rey**.)

SAN LUCAS
(ST LUKE)

Luke, to whom are attributed the third gospel and the Acts of the Apostles, was in 1842 honored in the title of a Mexican land grant that subsequently gave its name to today's small community of San Lucas in Monterey County. There are also a San Lucas Creek, in Santa Barbara County, and a San Lucas Canyon, in Inyo County.

It has been generally acknowledged that Luke's gospel, the longest of the four, is also the most poetic, graphic, and "artistic," for which reason he has become the patron saint of artists. This accounts for the unauthenticated tradition that he was himself an artist and painted a picture of the Virgin Mary. In fact, Luke was a Greek physician (he is with perfectly good sense the patron saint of doctors) who was born around the same time as Jesus. He never knew Jesus personally, however, but was a disciple of the Apostle Paul. Possibly because the element of sacrifice is stressed in his gospel, Luke's emblem is a (sometimes winged) steer or bull, a common sacrificial animal in Biblical times.

St Luke, with his emblem of a winged bull. Stained glass, 1955, by Judson Studios (Los Angeles). Chapel of the Dominican Sisters at Mission San Jose, Fremont, California.

SANTA LUCIA
(ST LUCY)

Lucy (Spanish: Lucía) was in earlier days (and to a lesser degree today still is) a much-venerated saint, both as an early martyr of the Christian Church and, more particularly, as a patron of the blind. The navigator Vizcaíno, sailing up the coast of California in 1602, named the vast Santa Lucia Range of mountains, in San Luis Obispo and Monterey Counties, after her about the time of her feast day of December 13. The little settlement of Lucia, a convenient stopping place on Highway 1, now lies on the coast at the foot of those mountains in Monterey County. There are also a Santa Lucia Canyon, in Santa Barbara County, and a Santa Lucia Wilderness in Los Padres National Forest.

The historical Lucy was a Sicilian girl martyred by the Romans for her faith. Many legends attach to her, including being consigned to a brothel as punishment for being a Christian, and having her eyes put out (later miraculously restored by St Peter). She was put to death by the sword around the year 304. Most likely, Lucy's link with eyes arises through a pun, her name, derived from the Latin *lux* (light), suggesting vision or light. She is generally shown in art holding her eyes on a plate.

St Lucy. Polychrome ceramic, 1920s, by Dal Prato Statuary. Sts Peter and Paul Church, San Francisco, California.

SAN LUIS
(ST ALOYSIUS)

San Luis Creek and Hill, in Merced County, were named for the Italian St Aloysius (Spanish: Luís) Gonzaga. A location in present-day Merced County first received the name from an expedition sent out from San Francisco presidio, the site having been discovered on June 21, 1805, the saint's feast day. Creek and hill were then named after the place.

Aloysius Gonzaga was born into one of Italy's most distinguished families in 1568. Though apparently destined for a life of power, wealth, and comfort, he renounced all of this and defied his father by becoming a Jesuit when aged twenty. Of an intense religiosity but a weak constitution, he insisted, against the will of his superiors, on nursing people sick of the plague in Rome in 1591. Though he became infected himself, he survived the plague, but died, much weakened from his exertions, later in the same year at the age of twenty-three. Aloysius is a patron saint of young people.

St Aloysius Gonzaga. Stained glass. Church of St Monica, San Francisco, California.

SAN LUIS OBISPO
(ST LOUIS THE BISHOP)

Louis (Spanish: Luís) the Bishop is one of the numerous Franciscan saints commemorated in California. Father Juan Crespí, accompanying Portolá's "Sacred Expedition," named the locality of the present city of San Luis Obispo in 1769, two days after the saint's feast day of August 19, and Junípero Serra founded the mission there in 1772 as California's fifth. It was the first mission to receive a tiled roof, a requisite component of California mission architecture today. Many other features are named for the bishop saint in San Luis Obispo County: San Luis Obispo Bay, Creek, and Peak, and San Luis Point, Canyon, Hills, and Range, as well as Port San Luis. San Luisito ("little San Luis") Creek is near the city.

Louis the Bishop, also known as Louis of Toulouse or Louis of Anjou, was, interestingly, a relative of St Louis of France (see next entry). Born the son of the King of Naples in 1274, Louis's life was shaped by seven years of his youth being spent as a hostage of war in Barcelona, Spain. During this time, he was educated by Franciscan friars, which resulted in his joining the order himself when he was released from bondage. In the same year as his ordination (1297), he was (thanks to his high social rank) appointed Bishop of Toulouse in France. Modest, self-effacing, and humble, he resigned his post almost immediately, however, and died in the same year at the early age of twenty-three.

St Louis the Bishop. Polychrome wood, mid-eighteenth century, from Mexico City. With kind permission of Mission San Luis Obispo, San Luis Obispo, California.

SAN LUIS REY
(ST LOUIS THE KING)

San Luis Rey is named for a saint who was both a king and a Franciscan tertiary (lay affiliate of the order). Mission San Luís Rey de Francia (King of France), in San Diego County, was founded in 1798 as the eighteenth of California's missions and was the last to be established by Father Lasuén as Franciscan President. He gave it the name at the behest of the Spanish Vice-Roy of New Spain, who wished in this way to mark the dynastic links between the Bourbon monarchies of Spain and France. Known as the "King of the Missions," San Luis Rey became Alta California's largest in the early years of the nineteenth century. Its church could hold a thousand worshipers, and it owned more cattle, sheep, and horses than any other mission. Today both a community and a river are named for the saint.

Louis IX of France (1214–70) is one of those royal saints of whom there lived not a few. As far as one can judge, he was a good king who genuinely cared for the welfare of his subjects. It was during his reign that the Sorbonne and many of France's Gothic cathedrals were constructed. When he acquired what was believed to be the Crown of Thorns with which Jesus was tormented before his crucifixion, he built the splendid Sainte-Chapelle in Paris specially to house it. A participant in the calamitous Seventh Crusade of 1248–54, he died of typhoid fever at Tunis, North Africa when on his way to the Eighth Crusade.

St Louis of France. Polychrome plaster. Church of San Francisco, Guanajuato, Mexico. Louis holds the Crown of Thorns on a cushion.

MOUNT MADONNA

Mount Madonna, in Santa Clara County, received its name, possibly from some Italian woodcutters, in the late nineteenth century. Mary as the Madonna with the baby Jesus is surely one of the most familiar and popular portrayals of the Virgin in Christian art. (See **Saint Mary**).

SAN MANUEL
(ST MANUEL)

In San Bernardino County there is a San Manuel Indian Reservation called after a nineteenth-century Indian tribal leader, Santos Manuel. The name is, therefore, at one remove from the original saint, as is the case with several other sites in the state. Manuel was, and still is, a popular name in Spain. Its popularity, however, is most likely due not to its reference to a saint, but because it is a short form for Emmanuel (Hebrew: "God is with us"), the name to be given to the Messiah according to Matthew 1: 23.

Manuel was a Persian saint of the fourth century. He was sent as an envoy for peace by the King of Persia to the pagan Byzantine Emperor Julian the Apostate. Julian killed him and several others when he discovered they were Christians.

In San Luis Obispo County there is an unpopulated location called Santa Manuela. It received the name through a land grant of 1836 and memorializes the Christian name of the wife of the original landowner, Francis Ziba Branch. One should regard Manuela simply as the feminine form of Manuel, with no correspondence to an actual historical or legendary saint.

Martydom of St Manuel. Fifteenth century, by Francesco dei Franceschi. Museo Correr, Venice, Italy. Courtesy of Cameraphoto Arte, Venice / Art Resource, NY.

SAN MARCOS
(ST MARK)

Mark the Evangelist was early commemorated in California. Though the city of San Marcos, in northern San Diego County, was not developed until after 1887, its name goes back to the San Marcos Valley, documented already in 1797. There are nearby also a San Marcos Creek, Lake, and Mountains. San Marcos Creek in San Luis Obispo County was actually recorded as early as 1795, while San Marcos Pass, between Solvang and Santa Barbara, in Santa Barbara County, was named for a ranch mentioned in 1817.

Mark's gospel, the second in the New Testament, was in fact the first to be completed (around the years 65 to 70). Though there is no actual evidence to prove it, its authorship is attributed to that historical Mark who, without knowing Jesus personally, knew Peter and Paul well and heard the gospel story from them. Mark traveled in Egypt, Cyprus, and Italy preaching the word, and it was in Alexandria, Egypt that he died in the year 74. In the ninth century, his relics were removed to Venice, where they rest today in the Basilica of San Marco. Various rather obscure links between Mark and a lion occur in his tradition, resulting in his emblem being a (usually winged) lion.

St Mark, with his lion. Oil on wood panel. Under pulpit
of Templo de Belén, Guanajuato, Mexico.

SANTA MARGARITA
(ST MARGARET)

Christian history and tradition know a number of St Margarets, two of whom are memorialized in California. The Santa Margarita River, in San Diego and Riverside Counties, was named in 1769 for Margaret of Antioch when Portolá and his men camped in its vicinity on her feast day of July 20. There are Santa Margarita Mountains in the same counties, too, while the name occurs also in Orange and Marin Counties.

Margaret of Antioch was a legendary saint. She was supposedly the daughter of a pagan priest of Antioch, Syria, but converted to Christianity. Rejected by her family, she lived for a time as a shepherdess. Then, refusing to marry the Roman governor of Antioch, she was imprisoned and tortured in various spectacular ways.

When in prison, legend relates, she was swallowed alive by a dragon, which, however, burst asunder so that Margaret escaped unscathed. This imagery accounts for her patronage of women in childbirth, which made her a much-invoked saint in the past.

St Margaret of Antioch, with her dragon. Statue on bridge over Walster River on Pilgrims' Way from Vienna to Mariazell, near Mariazell, Austria.

The small country town of Santa Margarita and Santa Margarita Creek and Lake, in San Luis Obispo County, hearken back to names that occur in Anza's diary in 1776. Gudde (347) explains that the name in this case was originally given by the padres of Mission San Luis Obispo and refers not to Margaret of Antioch, but to Margaret of Cortona, to whom today's church in Santa Margarita is dedicated.

Margaret of Cortona (1247–96) was an Italian Franciscan lay-woman known for her penances and charities. As a young woman she lived for nine years with a nobleman lover, to whom she bore a son. When her lover was murdered, she was rejected by her family and society and had to endure many insults and hardships. After she became a Franciscan ter-tiary, her dedication to the poor and the sick, and her reputedly miraculous cures, earned her a saintly reputation. According to tradition, Margaret was led to the grave of her mur-dered lover by her little dog, which is her emblem.

St Margaret of Cortona, with her dog. Oil on canvas, 1995, by Fr Sebastian Scicluma O.F.M. Parish church of Santa Margarita, San Luis Obispo County, California.

123

SANTA MARIA
(ST MARY)

There is lack of unanimity about the inspiration for the name Santa Maria (Spanish: María) in California. While Sanchez (110) claims that it derives from the Virgin Mary, Gudde (347) asserts, more persuasively, that it refers not to Jesus's mother (designated as Nuestra Señora in California), but to some other saint, such as Mary Magdalene. Whatever the case, as Santa Barbara County's most northerly town, Santa Maria, laid out around 1874, takes its name from a Mexican land grant of 1837. There are a Santa Maria Valley and River in the same county, while the river runs also in San Luis Obispo County. Santa Maria Creek and Valley, in San Diego County, received their names from a land grant of 1843.

Mary the mother of Jesus is discussed at various points in this book, but a word will be in order here on Mary Magdalene. Named for her native town of Magdala near the Sea of Galilee, Mary was the most prominent of Jesus's women followers. She is traditionally seen as the quintessential penitent, being identified with the unnamed sinner in scripture who washed Jesus's feet with her tears, dried them with her hair, anointed them with unguent, and whom Jesus pardoned. Mary Magdalene was present at the crucifixion and was the first person to see Jesus after his resurrection. She has often been depicted by artists – for example, by Giotto, Duccio, Caravaggio, Guercino, Piero di Cosimo, El Greco, and Quentin Massys. In art she is recognizable by her beautiful long hair and her pot of ointment.

St Mary Magdalene. Stained-glass window, 2002, by David Goines.
Church of St Mary Magdalen, Berkeley, California.

SAN MARINO
(ST MARINUS)

The prosperous city of San Marino, adjacent to Pasadena in Los Angeles County, is only obliquely connected with the historical St Marinus. Its name actually comes from a mansion that itself was called after a place in Maryland named for the tiny Italian city-republic of San Marino. California's San Marino is the home of the Henry E. Huntington Library and Art Gallery, established in 1919.

Marinus was a third-century stonemason who worked at Monte Titano, the site of a once important quarry near San Marino on Italy's Adriatic coast. There, while still a layman, he preached to Christians whom the Romans had sentenced for their faith to hard labor in the quarry. He later became a priest, but retired from society to live as a hermit when falsely accused by an insane woman of being her husband. Tradition has it that he founded the city of San Marino in 301.

St Marinus. Fresco, early sixteenth century, by School of Ghirlandaio.
Courtesy of the Museo di Stato della Repubblica di San Marino.
The saint holds the city he is said to have founded.

SAN MARTIN
(ST MARTIN)

One of the earliest Spanish-named locations in all California was Cape San Martin (Spanish: Martín), attached to a point on the coast near today's Big Sur by the navigator Juan Rodríguez Cabrillo. This happened on St Martin's Day, November 11, 1542. After being "lost" for centuries, the name was revived in 1870 and restored by the Coast Survey to a promontory at least near to Cabrillo's original Cape San Martin. The town of San Martin, in Santa Clara County, has a quite unrelated origin. It was called after a property thus named around 1844 by the landowner Martin Murphy in honor of his patron saint, Martin of Tours.

St Martin, born around 316 in the Roman province of Pannonia (today's Hungary), was a soldier in the Roman army until a mystical experience changed his life forever. When on a tour of duty in Amiens, France, he one winter's day supposedly cut his cloak in half to share with an almost naked beggar. A dream then revealed to him that the beggar had been Jesus. Martin subsequently became a hermit near Poitiers, France and evangelized much of the surrounding area. Such was his reputation for goodness and piety that in 372 he was appointed Bishop of Tours, which he remained for the last twenty-five years of his life.

St Martin. Stone high-relief, sixteenth century, by Isidro Villoldo. Above portal of Casa de la Misericordia, Ávila, Spain.

SAINT MARY

There are a Saint Marys Creek in Lake County, a Saint Marys Pass in Alpine County, and a Saint Marys Peak in Merced County. This being the English form of Mary's name, one may assume that, unlike Santa Maria (see above), it refers to the Virgin rather than some other Mary.

As the mother of Jesus, this saint scarcely needs an introduction. Her story is familiar from the gospels, though one might mention just a few key points in her life as they relate to Jesus: the Annunciation, the Visitation, the Nativity, the Flight into Egypt, the Presentation in the Temple, and the Crucifixion. Her fate after the crucifixion is uncertain, though it is possible that she died in Ephesus, Greece around the year 48. She is perhaps best loved in her depiction with the Christ Child, or with her husband Joseph and Jesus (Holy Family).

St Mary. (Our Lady of China). Polychrome wood and plaster, 1930s. Paulist Fathers, Holy Family Chinese Mission/Cathedral of Old St Mary's, San Francisco, California. Made in Italy for a Hong Kong church and brought to San Francisco *c.*1938, this statue shows Mary and the infant Jesus with Asian features, indicating how saintly depictions may be influenced by their physical and social context and at the same time stressing the universality of the Christian message.

SAN MATEO
(ST MATTHEW)

The name of Matthew the Evangelist was attached to a creek, in today's San Mateo County, by Anza in 1776 and was extended to a settlement in the 1790s. The county was created in 1856, and the modern city, a residential community on the San Francisco Peninsula, was established in 1863. In the county, too, are San Mateo Point and Slough. The San Mateo Bridge, one of the two major South Bay crossings, was built in 1929. There are also a San Mateo Creek, Canyon, Point, and Rocks in San Diego County. Of these, the creek was mentioned as early as 1778.

Matthew was a tax gatherer for the Romans (a much despised occupation among the Jews) before he was called to be a disciple of Jesus. The gospel attributed to him stresses Jesus's human connections and family lineage through Jewish kings. For this reason, Matthew's emblem as an evangelist is a man, or a winged man (i.e., an angel).

St Matthew Writing His Gospel. Oil on canvas, *c.*1670s, by Carlo Dolci. Courtesy of the J. Paul Getty Museum, Los Angeles, California.

MERCED
(MERCY)

The earliest application of Merced to a California site was in San Francisco County's Lake Merced. It was named for Nuestra Señora de la Merced (Our Lady of Mercy) by members of the Anza expedition who camped there in 1775, near her feast day of September 24. Later, on an 1806 tour of exploration from San Francisco presidio, Lieutenant Gabriel Moraga and his men gave the name to the Merced River, in today's Merced County, five days after her feast day. Sanchez (8) comments on the name's aptness, as it was surely a "mercy" for the soldiers to find this stream of fresh water after crossing forty miles of hot, dry valley. The county and the city of Merced were established in 1855 and 1872 respectively. Also in Merced County are Merced Peak, Pass, and Lake, as well as Merced Grove of giant sequoias and the small community of Merced Falls.

As the most important of the saints, Mary appears in many ideal guises – for example, as Our Lady of Perpetual Help, Our Lady Queen of the Sea, Our Lady of Grace, of the Snows, of Good Counsel, etc. An order of Mercedarians, whose patron is Our Lady of Mercy, was established in Spain in 1218 and dedicated to ransoming Christian captives from the Moors. In her role as Our Lady of Mercy, Mary may appear as "Protectress," sheltering humanity under her cloak, or may bear the chains of released prisoners.

Schutzmantelmadonna (Our Lady of Mercy). Wood high relief, *c.*1520, painted in twentieth century. Cathedral of Eichstätt, Germany.

SAN MIGUEL
(ST MICHAEL)

San Miguel Island, one of the four Santa Barbara Islands, in Santa Barbara County, was discovered for Spain in 1542 by the navigator Cabrillo, who is thought by some historians to have been buried there, though his grave has not been discovered. The island did not receive its present name until about 1790, however. San Miguel Channel separates it from Santa Rosa Island.

Father Lasuén, at the time Franciscan President, founded Mission San Miguel Arcángel (the Archangel) in 1797 as the sixteenth of California's missions. Both the mission and the adjacent community of San Miguel are in San Luis Obispo County, which also has a San Miguel Canyon. The mission was severely damaged in an earthquake in 2003.

San Diego County has a San Miguel Mountain, whose name dates from 1843, while Santa Barbara County has a San Miguelito ("little San Miguel") Creek.

Michael, perennially one of the most popular of saint's names, refers to the Archangel Michael, the commander of the Heavenly Host that cast Satan out of Paradise. He is also the gatekeeper of heaven, who weighs in his scales the souls of the dead for admission to paradise or expulsion to hell. As God's commander, he is, with George, a patron saint of soldiers, but on account of his scales he is also, somewhat humorously, the patron saint of greengrocers.

St Michael. Polychrome wood reredos, sixteenth century. With kind permission of Mission San Fernando Rey, Mission Hills, California.

SANTA MONICA
(ST MONICA)

It is a paradox of historical development that St Monica (Spanish: Mónica), the mother of St Augustine (see under **San Agustin**), today enjoys greater prominence among California's place names than does her otherwise more celebrated son. The Santa Monica Mountains, in Los Angeles County, were probably named by the Portolá expedition as early as 1770 on Monica's feast day of May 4, according to the old calendar. The name was applied to the modern city, on Santa Monica Bay, when it was begun in 1875, while there is, too, a Santa Monica Canyon in Los Angeles County. West of Carpinteria, in Santa Barbara County, there is a Santa Monica Creek.

Monica is regarded as a model for Christian mothers, whose patron saint she is. All her early prayers and efforts were directed toward the conversion to a pious life of her unbelieving son Augustine, who, of course, ultimately did become a Christian and was baptized when thirty-three years old. She kept his company whenever she could, even at the various stations of his pre-conversion life in Rome and Milan. She was accompanying him home to North Africa after his conversion when she died at the age of fifty-five in 387.

St Monica. Icon, 2000, by Sister Marie-Paul Farran, O.S.B. Church of St Monica, Santa Monica, California.

SAN NICOLAS
(ST NICHOLAS)

Though Nicholas (Spanish: Nicolás) has become a cultural cliché as the patron of children in his guise as Santa Claus, it is less well known that he is also a patron saint of sailors. Hence the appositeness of the navigator Vizcaíno's naming today's San Nicolas Island, in Ventura County, after him on his feast day of December 6, 1602. It is one of the Catalina Islands.

The historical Nicholas was a fourth-century Bishop of Myra, in today's Turkey. His patronage of children derives from two of the many legends attached to him. He is reputed to have saved three girls from a life of prostitution by providing them with three bags or balls of gold as a dowry. And he is also supposed to have saved three boys from being boiled alive in a tub of brine by a butcher. His patronage of sailors, which he shares with some other saints, stems from the legend that he miraculously rescued some drowning seamen from a sinking ship.

St Nicholas, with his three gold balls and the three boys he rescued. Oil on canvas.
Parish church of Bucerias, Nayarit, Mexico.

SAN ONOFRE
(ST ONOPHRIUS)

Onophrius is portrayed in art as a hirsute, desert-dwelling hermit, suiting him well enough to the topography of southern California in Spanish times. The earliest mention of his name occurs around 1795, when applied to the Cañada San Onofre, in present day Santa Barbara County. Today the saint's name is attached to a creek, canyon, mountain, hill, and bluff, in San Diego County. There are also a San Onofre State Beach and a San Onofre Nuclear Generating Station (established in 1968) in the same county.

Onophrius (which can be rendered as Humphrey in English) was a third-century hermit who lived for seventy years in the desert near Thebes in Upper Egypt. He is reputed to have survived on the fruit of a date tree and a palm tree growing close to his hermitage. He enjoyed some popularity in medieval Europe, first among monks, then, interestingly, as the patron saint of weavers. The reason for this is that he was said to have covered himself only with his own hair and with a loincloth woven from leaves. He died around the year 400.

St Onophrius. Detail of *Elkofener Altar*, oil on wood panel, 1517–20, by Meister von Rabenden and his School. Courtesy of the Bayerisches Nationalmuseum, Munich, Germany.

SAN PABLO
(ST PAUL)

The name of the great apostle and missionary Paul attaches to a number of important features in Contra Costa County. San Pablo Point, in San Francisco Bay, was named around 1811. The northeastern reach of San Francisco Bay is called San Pablo Bay, and the city of San Pablo was first mentioned around 1851. There are also a San Pablo Strait, Creek, Reservoir, and Dam in Contra Costa County.

It would be difficult to exaggerate Paul's importance for the emergence and establishment of the Christian Church. Born a Jew in Tarsus, in today's Turkey, around the year 10, he had, in fact, been a persecutor of Christians until, traveling on the road from Jerusalem to Damascus, he was struck from his horse by a bolt of lightening and heard the voice of Jesus speak to him. This resulted in his sudden conversion. Paul's vital contribution to the Church was his extension of the news of redemption beyond the Jews to the Gentiles. He brought this message on missionary journeys to communities throughout the Mediterranean world. Subsequently he wrote letters to the young Christian churches, and these constitute a major part of the New Testament. When he was visiting Rome, he was executed by beheading as a Christian under the Emperor Nero in the year 65.

Paulussturz (The Conversion of St Paul). Oil on canvas, *c.*1527–28, by Parmigianino.
Courtesy of the Kunsthistorisches Museum, Vienna.

SAN PASQUAL
(ST PASCAL OR PASCHAL)

Pascal Baylon, though nowadays a virtually forgotten saint, would, as a Spanish Franciscan, have been well known to California's missionaries. The name of today's small community of San Pasqual, set among idyllic citrus groves, and of the adjacent valley and Indian Reservation in San Diego County, stems from Spanish times. A battle between the Mexicans and the Americans took place in the area in 1846.

Born in Torrehermosa, Spain in 1540, Pascal Baylon was in his youth a shepherd boy who had to teach himself to read and write without the benefit of schooling. First rejected by the Franciscans when he tried to join their order, he was finally accepted as a lay brother. This meant that he was excluded from the cloistered, contemplative life of the other monks in order to fulfill more mundane and menial duties. He spent most of his life as a gatekeeper in various Spanish monasteries. However, he became known for his devotion to the sick and needy, and for his charities and mortifications, and was reputed to possess miraculous powers. He died at the priory in Villareal in 1592. In art he is shown as a Franciscan with sheep, an allusion to his days as a shepherd.

St Pascal Baylon. Cathedral of Zacatecas, Mexico.

SANTA PAULA
(ST PAULA)

The attractive Ventura County town of Santa Paula, founded in 1872, recalls that Paula who was a close associate of St Jerome (see under **San Geronimo**). The name actually goes back in the area to a ranch of Mission San Buenaventura recorded in 1834. It has been given also to a neighboring creek and canyon, as well as to a peak and ridge in Los Padres National Forest.

Born of a prominent Roman family in 347, Paula went through a religious conversion after the early death of her husband and one of her daughters. She then donated much of her wealth to the poor and lived a life of austerity and penance. In 385, however, she left Rome with some other women, including her own daughter St Eustochium, and followed St Jerome to the Holy Land. Here she assisted him in his New Testament studies both financially and through her knowledge of Greek. She died in Jerusalem in the year 404, about the time Jerome's translation of the Bible was completed.

The Holy Trinity with Sts Jerome, Paula, and Eustochium. Fresco, c.1455, by Andrea del Castagno. Basilica of Santissima Annunziata, Florence, Italy.
Courtesy of Scala/Art Resource, NY.

SAN PEDRO
(ST PETER)

San Pedro Bay, in Los Angeles County, surveyed for Spain by Vizcaíno in 1602, probably received its name because it was sighted on November 26, the feast day of that St Peter who was a Bishop of Alexandria martyred in 311. He is interesting as the last Christian to have been martyred by the Romans in that city. The name was later applied to San Pedro Channel, Hill, and Hills, as well as to the harbor community that since 1909 has been part of the city of Los Angeles.

Point San Pedro, in Marin County, mentioned as early as 1811, is situated opposite Point San Pablo of Contra Costa County, and hence no doubt refers to the great Apostle Peter, who is frequently linked with Paul. There are in San Mateo County also a Pedro Point, Creek, Valley, and Hill, going back to a rancho of Mission Dolores of 1791.

Peter (the name means "rock" in Greek) enjoys preeminence among the disciples because Jesus called him the "rock upon whom he would build his Church" (Matthew 16: 18–19). In the eyes of Catholics, this effectively created him the first Pope. Jesus also symbolically gave him the keys of the kingdom of heaven, for which reason crossed keys (or a key) are one of the saint's emblems, while crossed keys are part of the papal coat-of-arms. In the Bible, Peter emerges as a fierce defender of Jesus (when he cuts off an ear of the high priest's servant upon Jesus's arrest), and yet as having wholly human failings (as when he three times denies his Lord). After the crucifixion, he preached the gospel in various parts of the Mediterranean area, ultimately in Rome, whose first bishop he became. Here, too, he was crucified under the Emperor Nero about the year 65. Above his tomb was built St Peter's Basilica, the foremost church in Christendom.

St Peter. Polychrome wood. Church of St Monica, San Francisco, California.

PURÍSIMA CONCEPCIÓN
(IMMACULATE CONCEPTION)

The Immaculate Conception is not merely a theological concept, but is also a name applied, like so many others, to the Virgin Mary. It refers to the belief that Mary was conceived without original sin – not that she conceived Jesus "immaculately," as is sometimes erroneously thought. The Franciscans cultivated a special devotion to the Immaculate Conception, a theological underpinning for which was provided by the Franciscan scholar Duns Scotus (*c.* 1265–1398). The Vatican did not formally declare the doctrine until 1854, however.

Father Lasuén founded Mission Purísima Concepción, in today's Santa Barbara County, on December 8, 1787, the Feast of the Immaculate Conception. It was California's elev-

enth mission. Like San Antonio de Padua, today's (reconstructed) mission buildings, in a charming and secluded setting, convey an excellent impression of how they might have looked in Spanish times. The name was extended from the mission to Purisima Point, Hills, and Canyon, also in Santa Barbara County. Purisima Creek, in San Mateo County, hearkens back to an Indian village named there in 1786.

Mary, the Immaculate Conception.
Polychrome wood, most likely eighteenth-century Mexican (restored) With kind permission of Carmel Mission, Carmel, California.

SAN QUENTIN
(ST QUENTIN)

Interestingly, San Quentin Point, on San Francisco Bay and in Marin County, was first called simply Punta de Quintín after an Indian outlaw Quintín who was captured there in 1824. United States authorities added the "San" later, in uniformity with similar names, while the spelling was changed to the more usual English form of Quentin. Today's community of San Quentin stands on the point, as does also San Quentin Penitentiary, the largest state penitentiary in California.

Though St Quentin's origins are unauthenticated, he was possibly born in Rome the son of a Roman senator. Upon his conversion to Christianity, he went as a missionary to Gaul (today's France), where he settled in Amiens and, as his *vita* relates, performed many miracles. Because of his evangelizing zeal he was arrested, tortured, and in 287 beheaded by the Roman authorities in the town now known in his honor as Saint-Quentin.

St Quentin. Cathedral of Saint-Quentin, France. One sees on Quentin's right shoulder one of the pegs that were driven into his body to torture him.

SAN RAFAEL
(ST RAPHAEL)

Franciscan padres gave the apt name of the Archangel Raphael (which in Hebrew means "God heals") to the mission they intended as a hospital for sick Indians from Mission San Francisco. Mission San Rafael Arcángel, in Marin County, founded by Father Sarría in 1817 as the second-last of California's twenty-one missions, now stands in the modern city of San Rafael, established around 1841. Nearby are San Rafael Bay, Rock, and Creek.

The San Rafael Mountains, which include the San Rafael Wilderness, are part of Los Padres National Forest in Santa Barbara County, while there are also San Rafael Hills in Los Angeles County.

Raphael is one of the three archangels named in the Bible and figures prominently in the apocryphal Old Testament Book of Tobit. Here, Tobit himself, a pious Jew, tells his life story. He had been blind, but was cured of his blindness through the miraculous application of the gall of a fish. A major part of his story is taken up by the account of a journey on foot undertaken by Tobit's son Tobias in the company of Raphael and a little dog. On Raphael's instructions, Tobias had caught the fish that was then used to effect wondrous cures.

St Rafael. Oil on canvas, *c.*1820, by an anonymous Chumash artist at Mission Santa Inés, Solvang, California. The saint is depicted with Native American features. Photograph by G. Aldana. Courtesy of the J. Paul Getty Museum, Los Angeles, California.

SAN RAMON
(ST RAYMOND)

The city of San Ramon (Spanish: Ramón), in Contra Costa County, dating from the 1850s, was called after a site known earlier simply as Ramon, the name of a local shepherd. The "San" was added later in conformity with similar California place names. There are also a creek and a valley bearing the name in the same county.

We do not know for which of two prominent St Raymonds the shepherd Ramon might have been named, Raymond of Pennafort (*c*.1180–1275) or Raymond Nonnatus (*c*.1204–40), both Spaniards.

The first of these was a Dominican friar who became Master-General of his order. He is known for a picturesque legend. The story goes that, when on the island of Mallorca, he quarreled with King James of Aragon over the latter's wickedness. Swearing he would no longer remain on the island with the king, Raymond sailed for six hours on his own outspread cloak across the sea to Barcelona.

The other Raymond received the cognomen Nonnatus (Latin: *non natus* = not born) because he was supposedly delivered by caesarean section from his dead mother. He early became a member of the Mercedarian Order, founded in 1218 for the ransom of Christian slaves or prisoners held by the Moors – an important function at that period of history. To this end, Raymond visited Algeria and, when his money ran out, offered himself in place of one or more captives, being released only months later. He was appointed a cardinal in 1239, but died just one year later. Because of the circumstances of his birth, he is a patron saint of midwives.

St Raymond Nonnatus. Templo de la Merced, Queretero, Mexico. Raymond wears the vestments of the Mercedarian Order. The chain refers to his freeing of prisoners.

SAN RAMON NONATO

POINT REYES
(KINGS' POINT)

Point Reyes, in Marin County, was so named by Vizcaíno because he sighted it from his ship on January 6, 1603, the day of the Three Kings (otherwise known as Epiphany). (See above under **Kings River and Canyon**).

SANTA RITA
(ST RITA)

Still much venerated today, Rita has given her name to a number of natural features and towns in California. Santa Rita Slough and Santa Rita Park community, in Merced County, bear names that go back in the area to around 1806, while Santa Rita Hills and Valley, in Santa Barbara County, derive their names from a Mexican land grant of 1839. The name occurs again in the community of Santa Rita, in Monterey County, and in Santa Rita Peak, in San Benito County.

Rita was born in 1377 in Roccaporena, Umbria and experienced a highly unsatisfactory married life. Her husband, a violent womanizer, was actually murdered in a feud, and her two sons, likewise violent individuals, died soon afterward, before they could avenge their father as they planned. Rita thereupon became an Augustinian nun, dedicating herself to penance and to the care of the sick and infirm. She was also a mystic, given to intense identification with the Passion of Jesus, so that a wound opened on her forehead as if pierced by the crown of thorns. Rita is a saint invoked in cases of marriage difficulties, accounting perhaps for the perennial importance of her cult.

St Rita. Polychrome wood head and hands, fabric on supporting frame, early seventeenth century. Real Parroquia de Santa María Magdalena, Seville, Spain.

SAN ROQUE
(ST ROCH)

Roch, a notable and rather picturesque French saint, is commemorated in San Roque Creek and Canyon, in Santa Barbara County. The name stems from the Portolá expedition, which camped at the mouth of the creek on August 19, 1769, three days after the saint's feast day.

One still quite frequently sees representations of Roch in churches, though his main importance lies in the past as he was traditionally invoked against the plague. Roch was a native of Montpellier who after the death of his parents spent the rest of his life on pilgrimages. When on a pilgrimage to Rome, he caught and almost died of the plague near Piacenza, Italy. Lying sick for days in a forest, he was saved only through the miraculous intervention of a little dog that brought him bread rolls in its jaws. After his recovery, he is said to have cured sufferers of the plague and, probably, to have returned to Montpellier, where he is thought to have died around 1380.

St Roch, with his dog and pointing to a plague wound on his leg. Polychrome ceramic, 1920s. Del Prato Statuary. Sts Peter and Paul Church, San Francisco, California.

St Rose, with her crown of roses. Pine, acrylics, and tin, 2000, by Luis Tapia. Church of St Francis Solano, Rancho Santa Margarita, California.

SANTA ROSA
(ST ROSE)

According to Gudde (348), the name Santa Rosa, very frequent in California, usually refers to Rose of Lima, the first saint of the Americas, and it has been attached to Santa Rosa Island of the Santa Barbara group since 1774. At the same time, Gudde asserts that some locations (he does not specify which) may be named for the Italian Franciscan nun St Rose of Viterbo (1235–53).

Santa Rosa Creek, in Sonoma County, was supposedly named by a priest who in 1829 baptized in it an Indian girl he called Rosa for the feast day of Rose of Lima (August 23), when the baptism took place. The name then was applied to the present city, established in 1853. Its most famous landmark is the former home and garden of the horticulturalist Luther Burbank (1849–1926), who cultivated and named the Santa Rosa plum.

Santa Rosa Mountains, with Santa Rosa Mountain, lie in Riverside, San Diego, and Imperial Counties. There are also Santa Rosa Hills, in Santa Barbara County, and a Santa Rosa Creek, in San Luis Obispo County, as well as a Santa Rosa Indian Reservation in Kings County.

The daughter of Spanish parents, Rose was born in Lima, Peru in 1586. From her earliest years she aspired to become a nun, and when she turned twenty she entered the Third Order of St Dominic. She donned the habit of a Dominican nun and took a vow of perpetual virginity, but resided in a little hut she herself helped build in her parents' garden. A mystic, she was known for her ecstasies and her harsh self-imposed penances. It was, for example, her practice to wear an iron "crown of thorns" that she concealed under a garland of roses. Beyond this, she was known for her concern for the natives and black slaves of Lima. She died in 1617.

SANTA ROSALIA
(ST ROSALIE)

Santa Rosalia (Spanish: Rosalía) Mountain and Ridge, in Santa Cruz County, are named for a Sicilian saint whose sanctuary can be visited today on a hill not far from Palermo. Rosalie (*c.* 1130–60) was born of Sicilian nobility and in her youth withdrew as a hermit to a cave near her parents' home. Tradition relates that she was led to the cave by angels and that she lived there a life of austerity, prayer, and penance. In the seventeenth century, after she had appeared in a vision to a hunter, her relics were discovered and transported to Palermo, where the then raging plague miraculously abated. She is now the patron saint of Palermo, and also of Monterey's Sicilian fishermen. Each year in September (her feast day falls on the fourth day of the month) her statue is paraded from Monterey's San Carlos Cathedral (Royal Presidio Chapel) to the waterfront for the blessing of the fleet.

St Rosalie. Plaster on wood, 1935. San Carlos Cathedral
(Royal Presidio Chapel), Monterey, California.

SANTIAGO
(ST JAMES)

It is appropriate that St James as Santiago, the patron saint of Spain, is commemorated in a number of California locations. As early as 1769 Portolá gave the name to a tributary of the Santa Ana River, in Orange County. This occurred two days after James's feast day of July 25. There are also a Santiago Peak and Reservoir in the same county. Santiago Peak received its name officially in 1894, but is known locally as Old Saddleback. Kern County also has a Santiago Creek. (See under **Saint James**.)

SAN SEBASTIAN
(ST SEBASTIAN)

Sebastian (Spanish: Sebastián) is one of the most frequently portrayed of all saints in art, and Botticelli, Mantegna, El Greco, Rubens, and Dürer, among others, have painted him. Given the historical importance of his cult, it is somewhat surprising that the only feature to bear his name in California is San Sebastian Marsh, in Imperial County. Named by Anza in 1774, it in fact commemorates the saint only indirectly, as Anza's intention was to honor his native guide Sebastián Tarabal.

Who does not know St Sebastian, that partly nude youth tied to a tree, with arrows sticking in him like a pincushion? (This accounts for his bizarre patronage of pin makers, as well as of archers.) In former times, Sebastian was fervently invoked against the dreaded plague, which was said to strike as swiftly as an arrow. His mostly legendary life story relates that he was a Roman soldier who around the year 300 was martyred for his faith. He was used first for target practice by archers and then beaten to death with clubs.

St Sebastian. This interesting folk-art portrayal of Sebastian comes from Tepoztlan, Mexico. It is a detail from the cathedral gateway ornamented with varicolored corn seeds. This gateway is renewed each year.

167

SAN SIMEON
(ST SIMEON)

The pretty coastal settlement of San Simeon (Spanish: Simeón), in San Luis Obispo County, was named for a ranch of Mission San Miguel first mentioned around 1819. Near the community lies the former estate of newspaper baron William Randolph Hearst (1863–1951), now Hearst San Simeon State Historical Monument. There are also a San Simeon Bay, Point, Creek, Beach, and State Park. It is uncertain whether the name honors St Simeon of Jerusalem (as claimed by Gudde 344 and Hoover et al. 76) or St Simeon Stylites (as attested by Hanna 286).

The first of these saints was possibly a relative of Jesus and served for over forty years as Bishop of Jerusalem. He is credited with miracles, and was persecuted and martyred in the year 106 during the reign of the Roman Emperor Trajan.

Simeon Stylites was a more intriguing figure. Born in Syria in 390, he is renowned as the first so-called "pillar hermit." His life was one of penance and self-mortification. Seeking in various ways to withdraw from society, he achieved this, though only partially, in a strange way – by living on the top of a pillar, or more precisely a series of pillars, the last over thirty feet high, where he spent the last twenty years of his life. Here he would prostrate himself in prayer, but he was also visited and consulted by pilgrims and even by three different Byzantine emperors, which resulted in his sought-after isolation eluding him. He died atop his pillar in 459. Tennyson wrote a poem, "St Simeon Stylites" (1842), inspired by Simeon's life.

St Simeon Stylites. Byzantine mosaic, Basilica of San Marco, Venice, Italy. Courtesy of Werner Forman / Art Resource, NY.

SOLANO
See SAN FRANCISCO SOLANO

SOLEDAD
(SOLITUDE)

The city of Soledad, in Monterey County, takes its name from Mission Nuestra Señora de la Soledad (Our Lady of Solitude), referring to the loneliness, or desolation, of the Virgin Mary after the crucifixion of Jesus. More precisely, the location was reportedly so named in 1776 because a party of Spaniards, upon asking an Indian woman her name, understood her to have replied "Soledad" (Gudde 369). When Father Lasuén founded the mission in 1771, the thirteenth of California's twenty-one, it was named accordingly.

Soledad occurs also as a name for a canyon, mountain, and valley in San Diego County, for a canyon and pass in Los Angeles County, and for a mountain in Kern County.

Our Lady of Solitude is the patron saint of Oaxaca, Mexico. Leonard Cohen has written a song dedicated to her.

Our Lady of Solitude. Polychrome wood and textile, 1950s. With kind permission of Soledad Mission, Soledad, California.

San Estanislao

STANISLAUS
(ST STANISLAUS KOSTKA)

Stanislaus, occurring most notably in Stanislaus County, is, like San Jacinto, a California Spanish place name with a Polish dimension. It reportedly derives from an Indian chief of the region who was baptized under the Spanish name of Estanislao. He was educated at Mission San Jose, but in the years 1827–29 became one of the most troublesome, and successful, renegades against the Mexican authorities. There are also a Stanislaus National Forest and a scattered community of Stanislaus, in Tuolumne County, and a Stanislaus River, which is a major tributary of the San Joaquin. Alpine County has a Stanislaus Peak.

Paradoxically, St Stanislaus, too, like Estanislao, was a sort of rebel, though of a much gentler disposition. His character and career in many ways resemble those of the better-known Aloysius Gonzaga. Born in Rostkovo Castle of a Polish noble family in 1550, he was educated first by a private tutor, and then at fourteen was sent to the Jesuit College in Vienna. Here he attracted attention for his studiousness, piety, and self-mortifications. During an illness, he experienced visions and determined to become a Jesuit. Opposed in this by his father, who wished a secular career for his son, he walked a distance of some three hundred and fifty miles from Vienna to Rome, to be accepted into the order by its General. Self-imposed austerities had sapped his strength, however, and he was carried off by malaria at the age of eighteen. His life has been held up as a model for Catholic youth, for which reason he is a patron saint of students.

St Stanislaus Kostka. Polychrome wood and textile, 1940s. Jesuit Church, Toledo, Spain. One typically encounters Stanislaus, as here, in Jesuit churches as a young Jesuit novice bearing the Christ Child. Apparently, he had a mystical experience of Mary visiting him and placing the baby Jesus in his arms.

SANTA SUSANA
(ST SUSANNA)

In Los Angeles and Ventura Counties the name Santa Susana can be traced back as far as 1804. In addition to the community of the name in Ventura County, there are Santa Susana Mountains in Ventura and Los Angeles Counties, and a Pass and Tunnel in Los Angeles County.

Susanna was an early virgin martyr. A member of the Roman patriciate, she refused as a Christian to marry a relative of the pagan Emperor Diocletian – a serious offence at that time, as Diocletian was a dire persecutor of the early Church. As a consequence, she was denounced as a Christian and was beaten and beheaded in 295. Her home became the site of the church of Santa Susanna, which is the church of the American parish in Rome today.

St Susanna. Fresco, 1598, by Baldassare Croce. Church of Santa Susanna, Rome.
Courtesy of Foto Bellocchio, Rome.

SANTA TERESA
(ST TERESA)

The great Spanish mystic Teresa of Ávila has given her name, by way of a Mexican land grant of 1834, to Santa Teresa Hills and Santa Teresa Spring, in Santa Clara County. Paradoxically, then, as with Augustine, Thomas Aquinas, and Ignatius Loyola, she has, despite her historical stature, left only a modest mark on California's place names. It will be noted that none of these saints was Franciscan.

Teresa was a Carmelite nun, born in 1515 of a noble Spanish family in Ávila. Joining the Carmelites when only twenty, she soon became disenchanted with the worldly life of convents in her day and played a major, and often controversial and difficult, part in reforming her order. Beyond this, she was one of the most intellectual and spiritual women of her age. Deeply mystical, she recorded her visions in several books, including her *Autobiography* (1565). She died in 1582 in Alba de Tormes, Spain, where she is also buried. For her learning, she was in 1970 proclaimed a Doctor of the Church, the first woman saint thus honored.

St Teresa of Ávila. Serra Chapel. With kind permission of Mission San Juan Capistrano, San Juan Capistrano, California. The book and the pen allude to Teresa's status as a Doctor of the Church.

SAN TIMOTEO
(ST TIMOTHY)

The name of Timothy has been honored since 1830 in San Timoteo Canyon and Creek, in Riverside and San Bernardino Counties. Timothy is remembered for his close ties to the Apostle Paul, whom he accompanied on several missionary journeys. He also acted as Paul's representative to some of the early Christian communities in Thessalonica, Corinth, and Ephesus. He may have been the first bishop of Ephesus, where for his opposition to paganism he was martyred by being first stoned, then beaten to death with clubs, when he was reputedly eighty years old.

St Timothy. Icon, 1992, by Brother Robert Lentz O.F.M. St Timothy's School, San Mateo, California. Courtesy of Trinity Stores, Highlands Ranch, Colorado.

SAN TOMAS AQUINAS
(ST THOMAS AQUINAS)

The name of the intermittent San Tomas Aquinas (Spanish: Santo Tomás de Aquino) Creek, in Santa Clara County, goes back to the 1850s. Gudde (283–84 in the 1960 edn of his work) has justifiably found irony in the fact that the name of such an important philosopher and scholar should be applied to such a minor natural feature. It is tempting, though not obligatory, to attribute this to the fact that Thomas was a Dominican friar, not a Franciscan. Certainly, he was one of the outstanding members of his order.

Born near Aquino, Italy about 1225, Thomas did not always find his way easily through life. In particular, he had to defy the wishes of his nobleman father (who entertained high social ambitions for him) when he joined the Dominicans at the age of nineteen. He was also awkward and phlegmatic as a youth and had to suffer the taunts of his fellows, who called him the "dumb ox." Clumsy Thomas may or may not have been, but dumb he never was. Educated by the leading Dominican scholar of his day, Albert the Great, in Paris and Cologne, he later himself became a teacher in Europe's foremost schools, in Paris, Rome, Cologne, and Bologna. His theological thought, expressed in his *Summa theologica* (unfinished at his death in 1274), has remained central to Catholic discourse down to the present.

St Thomas Aquinas. Stained glass, 1958, by Merrill Stained Glass. Church of St Emydius, Lynwood, California. The radiant sun on his breast, bringing light to the Church, is Thomas's emblem.

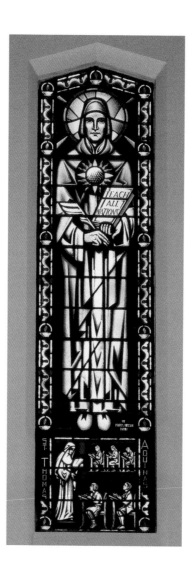

St Bonaventure. Polychrome wood. With kind permission of Mission
San Antonio de Padua, California.

VENTURA
(ST BONAVENTURE)

The name of St Bonaventure, the great Italian Franciscan friar and cardinal, was given to Mission San Buenaventura when Father Junípero Serra established it in 1782. Strategically situated between San Diego and Monterey, it was one of the three earliest missions planned (in 1769), but construction on it was continually postponed for financial and logistical reasons. It became the ninth of California's missions and the last founded by Serra. The city and county, dating from 1861 and 1872 respectively, were called after the mission, but their names were truncated (perhaps "mutilated" would be a better word) to Ventura later in the century. Similarly, the nearby river has been called the Ventura River since 1895.

Though less well known than Thomas Aquinas, whose contemporary he was, Bonaventure (1218–74) was, like him, one of the outstanding churchmen of his age. He was to the Franciscans what Thomas was to the Dominicans – a philosopher and theologian whose works are still read today. Unlike Thomas, however, he emphasized feeling, emotion, and the instincts, rather than reason, as a way to theological truths.

Beyond this, Bonaventure was a skilled organizer and has been called the second founder of the Franciscan Order, whose Minister-General he became when only thirty-six. His achievement was to reconcile conflicting trends in the order, which at the time was in danger of fragmenting due to the opposing forces of austerity and scholarship. Bonaventure stressed and exemplified simplicity of life (espoused by the more traditional Franciscans) without denying the importance of learning and teaching (which the more modern friars favored). For his sublime erudition, Bonaventure was known as the "Seraphic Doctor."

SAN VICENTE
(ST VINCENT)

The name San Vicente in California might possibly refer to a number of St Vincents. Its earliest occurrence, in Los Angeles County, dates from 1802, and there is today a mountain of the name in that county recorded since 1828. There are also San Vicente Creeks in Santa Cruz, San Diego, and San Mateo Counties.

Three St Vincents are particularly prominent. These are Vincent of Saragossa, Vincent Ferrer, and Vincent de Paul. Vincent of Saragossa is known primarily as the proto-martyr of Spain – i.e., as the earliest Spanish Christian to be martyred (in 304). Vincent Ferrer (1350–1419) was a Spanish Dominican celebrated as one of the great preachers of his age. He is also remembered as a preacher against Jews and heretics, however – an unattractive feature in our hopefully more enlightened age. Easy to admire on the other hand is Vincent de Paul (1581–1660), a French priest universally respected for his charities and devotion to the poor and needy, regardless of their religious affiliations. He founded schools, orphanages, and hospitals, and also worked for the ransom of Christian prisoners in Moorish captivity. The worldwide charitable St Vincent de Paul Society was named for him when founded in France in 1833.

St Vincent de Paul. Parish church of San Miguel de Allende, Mexico.

SAN
VICENTE DE PAUL

SANTA YNES (OR INÉS)
(ST AGNES)

Mission Santa Inés Virgen y Mártir, in the present-day town of Solvang in Santa Barbara County, was dedicated to the Italian martyr St Agnes when founded in 1804 by Father Estévan Tápis, the then President of the Franciscan missionaries. The nineteenth of California's twenty-one missions, it gave its name to the Santa Ynes River, Valley, Mountains, Peak, and Fault, the spelling Ynes having become current during the American era. The town of Santa Ynes in Santa Barbara County was founded in 1882.

Agnes was an early Roman martyr who died around 305. She provided an important role model for young girls in the past for her refusal to marry in order to dedicate herself as a virgin to God. The law of the Roman Empire, which demanded sacrifice to the pagan gods, sentenced her to death for her faith. She was stabbed in the neck with a dagger or sword. Because her name sounds like Latin *agnus* (= lamb), her emblem in art is a lamb.

St Agnes. Polychrome plaster. With kind permission of Old Mission Santa Inés, Solvang, California.

SANTA YSABEL
(ST ELIZABETH)

The small community of Santa Ysabel, in San Diego County, is named for St Elizabeth – most likely, as Gudde (350) suggests, Elizabeth of Portugal, who was born a Spanish princess in 1271. As a place name it has been recorded since 1818, when it was applied to a chapel of Mission San Diego. (A pretty little chapel stands near the original site today.) Santa Ysabel lies in the lovely valley of the same name, while there are also a Santa Ysabel Creek and Indian Reservation in the county.

St Elizabeth of Portugal. Church of La Merced, Morelia, Mexico.

Elizabeth was married at the tender age of twelve to King Denis of Portugal, who proved a profligate, unfaithful, and uncaring husband. Nevertheless, Elizabeth conducted herself as a model Christian queen and wife, even bringing up some of her husband's illegitimate offspring. In addition to this, she used her own wealth to build or support churches, monasteries, hospitals, and homes for orphans and abandoned women. After her husband's death, she became a Franciscan tertiary (lay affiliate of the order) and died in 1336. A legend relates that, when accused by her husband of smuggling food out of their palace for the poor, she opened the folds of her cloak to reveal not food, but roses. She may, therefore, be shown bearing food or roses in her cloak or apron.

SAN YSIDRO
(ST ISIDORE)

The name of the Spanish peasant-saint Ysidro has been in use in California since 1836, when it was applied to what was probably a ranch of Mission San Diego. San Ysidro is today a San Diego community and port of entry from Mexico. There are also a mountain, a creek, and two ridges of the name in San Diego County. There are San Ysidro Creeks in Santa Barbara, San Benito, and Santa Clara Counties.

Isidore the Farmer, as he is known, is the patron saint of Madrid, near which city he was born and lived his entire life (*c.*1080–1130) as a farm laborer. He was known for his piety, and many charming legends are told of him – for example, of angels plowing his fields for him while he prayed. He is also said to have miraculously discovered a spring while digging – accounting perhaps for the number of creeks named for him in California. After his death, other wonders were attributed to him, including the recovery of King Philip III of Spain from a deadly fever when Isidore's relics were brought into his sickroom. This led the king to petition successfully for Isidore's canonization in 1622.

St Isidore. Polychrome wood. With kind permission of
Mission San Buenaventura, Ventura, California.

SELECT BIBLIOGRAPHY

Attwater, Donald. *The Penguin Dictionary of Saints*. London and New York: Penguin Books, 1995.

Bancroft, Hubert Howe. *History of California*. 7 vols. Rept. Santa Barbara: Wallace Hebberd, 1963–70.

Bean, Walter. *California: An Interpretive History*. 2nd edn. New York: McGraw-Hill, 1973.

Beck, Warren A., and David A. Williams. *California: A History of the Golden State*. New York: Doubleday, 1972.

Bibliotheca Sanctorum. 12 vols. Rome: Istituto Giovanni XXIII, 1961–69.

The Book of Saints: A Comprehensive Biographical Dictionary. 7th edn., revised and reset. Ed. by Dom Basil Watkins, O.S.B. on behalf of the Benedictine monks of St Augustine's Abbey, Ramsgate. London: A. and C. Black, 2002.

Butler's Lives of the Saints. 4 vols. Ed., revised, and supplemented by Herbert J. Thurston and Donald Attwater. Westminister, Maryland: Christian Classics, 1981.

The California Missions: A Pictorial History. The Sunset Editors. Menlo Park: Sunset Books, 1997.

Columbian Consequences. Vol. 1. Ed. David Hurst Thomas. Washington: Smithsonian Institution, 1989.

Delaney, John J. *Dictionary of Saints*. New York: Doubleday, 1980.

Durham, David L. *California's Geographic Names: A Gazetteer of Historic and Modern Names of the State*. Clovis, California: Word Dancer Press, 1998.

Farmer, David Hugh. *The Oxford Dictionary of Saints*. 5th edn. Oxford and New York: Oxford University Press, 2003.

Gerhard, Peter. *The North Frontier of New Spain*. Rev. edn. Norman and London: University of Oklahoma Press, 1993.

Giorgi, Rosa. *Saints in Art*. Translated from the Italian by Thomas Michael Hartmann. Los Angeles: The John Paul Getty Museum, 2003.

Giorgi, Rosa. *Saints: A Year in Faith and Art*. New York: Abrams, 2006.

Gudde, Erwin G. *California Place Names: The Origin and Etymology of Current Geographical Names*. 2nd edn. Berkeley: University of California Press, 1960.

Gudde, Erwin G. *California Place Names: The Origin and Etymology of Current Geographical Names*. 4th edn., revised and enlarged by William Bright. Berkeley, Los Angeles, and London: University of California Press, 2004.

Guerrero, Vladimir. *The Anza Trail and the Settling of California*. Santa Clara: Santa Clara University Press, 2006; Berkeley: Heyday Books, 2006.

Guiley, Rosemary Ellen. *The Encyclopedia of Saints*. New York: Facts on File, 2001.

Hanna, Phil Townsend. *The Dictionary of California Land Names*. Los Angeles: Automobile Club of Southern California, 1951.

Hart, James D. *A Companion to California*. Berkeley, Los Angeles, and London: University of California Press, 1987.

Hoover, Mildred Brooke et al. *Historic Spots in California*. Rev. by Douglas E. Kyle. Stanford: Stanford University Press, 1990.

Internet resources. Countless relevant sites are accessible through the Internet, though they should be used with discretion. Most useful for art are: the Web Gallery of Art (http://www.wga.hu); Olga's Gallery (http://abcgallery. com.). For saints: Patron Saints Index (http://www.catholic-forum.com/saints/patron02.htm); the New Catholic Dictionary, 1910 edition (http:// www.catholicforum.com); the Catholic Encyclopedia, 1913 edition (http://www.newadvent.org). For California places: http://www.placenames.com/us/06/ ; http://www.epodunk.com/profiles/ca_a.html.

Lanzi, Fernando and Gioia. *Saints and Their Symbols: Recognizing Saints in Art and in Popular Images*. Translated from the Italian by Matthew J. O' Connell. Collegeville, Minnesota: The Liturgical Press, 2004.

Lavender, David. *California: Land of New Beginnings*. New York: Harper and Row, 1972.

Marinacci, Barbara and Rudy. *California's Spanish Place Names: What They Mean and the History They Reveal*. Santa Monica, California: Angel City Press, 2005.

McBrien, Richard P. *Lives of the Saints: From Mary and St Francis of Assisi to John XXIII and Mother Teresa*. San Francisco: Harper, 2001.

Metford, J. C. J. *Dictionary of Christian Lore and Legend*. London: Thames and Hudson, 1983.

Mornin, Edward and Lorna. *Saints: A Visual Guide*. London: Frances Lincoln, 2006; Grand Rapids, Michigan: William B. Eerdmans, 2006; Toronto: Novalis, 2006.

Murray, Peter and Linda. *A Dictionary of Christian Art*. Oxford: Oxford University Press, 2004.

Neuerburg, Norman. *Saints of the California Missions*. Santa Barbara: Bellerophon Books, 2001.

Sanchez, Nellie Van de Grift. *Spanish and Indian Place Names of California: Their Meaning and Their Romance*. San Francisco: A. M. Robertson, 1922.

Schauber, Vera, and Hanns Michael Schindler. *Heilige und Namenspatrone im Jahreslauf*. Augsburg: Pattloch Verlag, 1999.

de Voragine, Jacobus. *The Golden Legend*. New York: Arno Press, 1969.

Wagner, Henry Raup. "Saints' Names In California," *Historical Society of Southern California Quarterly*, vol. 29 (March 1947), 49–58.

Wimmer, Otto. *Kennzeichen und Attribute der Heiligen*. Revised and enlarged by Barbara Knoflach-Zingerle. Vienna and Innsbruck: Tyrolia-Verlag, 2000.

INDEX

Saints are in bold. *Page numbers indicating illustrations are in bold italics*.
Places are in italics. All other entries are in roman.

ACKNOWLEDGMENTS

It is our pleasant obligation to acknowledge here a number of people who have variously contributed to the making of this book. At the J. Paul Getty Museum our most sincere thanks go to Leslie Rollins, who has supported us in numerous substantial ways, and to Ruth Lane for her cheerful and effective assistance in obtaining permissions for us. At Frances Lincoln Publishers we wish to express our gratitude to John Nicoll for his continuing confidence in our work, and to Andrew Dunn for his tireless promotion of our book and for following its progress so conscientiously and constructively. Thanks also to Becky Clarke for her creative design work and to Anna Sanderson for her careful editing. Difficult to obtain images were generously provided for us by Luca Bellocchio (for Susanna), Alicja Rakuzyn (for Venantius), and Anna Simoncini (for Marinus). For allowing us to photograph their works, our gratitude is due also to the many churches named in our text, as well as to the following artists: Sister Marie-Paul Farran, David Goines, Thomas March, Lisa Reinertson, and Luis Tapia. Last but not least, we would like to express our special appreciation to our friends John Rengel and Marketa Goetz-Stankiewicz, whose enthusiasm and encouragement have been a great joy and support to us in the writing of this work.

Listed here are photographic sources acknowledged separately in the text:
Bayerisches Nationalmuseum, Munich
Dordrechts Museum, Dordrecht, Netherlands
Foto Bellocchio, Rome
The J. Paul Getty Museum, Los Angeles
Kunsthistorisches Museum, Vienna
Museo di Stato della Repubblica di San Marino, San Marino
National Gallery of Art, Dublin
Scala/Art Resource, New York
Trinity Stores, Highlands Ranch, Colorado